ANY BITCH CAN LOSE IT

AND WE MEAN THIS IN A GOOD WAY!

BABE IN TOTAL CONTROL OF HERSELF

I ALWAYS START MY DIET ON THE SAME DAY. TOMORROW!

ISBN 1-57166-582-X

PRINTED BY
JUMBO JACK'S COOKBOOKS
AUDUBON, IOWA

TABLE OF CONTENTS

NOTES

_____

_____

_____

_____

_____

_____

_____

_____

_____

_____

_____

_____

_____

_____

_____

_____

_____

BREAKFAST

AND

BREADS

NOTES

_____

_____

_____

_____

_____

_____

_____

_____

_____

_____

_____

_____

_____

_____

_____

_____

_____

SCRAMBLED EGG POCKETS

1/2 C. chopped tomato
1/4 C. chopped onion
2 T. chopped green bell pepper
2 C. egg substitute
1 t. chopped fresh tarragon

1/4 t. salt
2 pita breads, cut in half and
   opened to form pockets
1/2 C. alfalfa sprouts

Spray a non-stick skillet with non-stick cooking spray. Cook the tomato, onion and bell pepper over medium heat about 3 minutes, stirring occasionally, until onion is tender. Mix the egg substitute, tarragon and salt. Pour into the skillet. As mixture begins to set at the bottom and side, gently lift cooked portions with a spatula as that thin, uncooked portion can flow to bottom. Cook 3 to 5 minutes. Spoon into pita breads. Top with the alfalfa sprouts. Serves 4.

Nutritional Information: 195 Calories, 5 g Fat, 23 g Carbohydrate, 0 mg Cholesterol, 450 mg Sodium, 15 g Protein.

We'll be friends until we are old and senile. Then, we'll be NEW friends.

BREAKFAST IN A CUP

4 oz. reduced-fat loose sausage
1/4 C. chopped green bell pepper
1/4 C. chopped onion
1 C. egg substitute
1 large egg

1-4 oz. can sliced mushrooms,
   drained
1/2 C. shredded reduced-fat
   Cheddar cheese

Preheat oven to 350 degrees F. Coat a 6-cup muffin pan with non-stick spray. In a non-stick skillet over medium-high heat, cook the sausage, pepper and onion 5 minutes or until sausage is done. Spoon the mixture in a bowl and cool slightly. Stir in the egg substitute, egg and mushrooms. Spoon mixture evenly into the pan. Sprinkle with the cheese. Bake for 20 minutes. Serves 6.

Nutritional Information: 107 Calories, 5 g Fat, 4 g Carbohydrate, 49 mg Cholesterol, 318 mg Sodium, 12 g Protein, 1 g Fiber.

*Somebody said being a mother is boring.....That somebody
never rode in a car driven by a teenager with a driver's permit.*

ARTICHOKE OMELET

1/4 C. sliced green onions, white part only, reserve green portion
3 cloves garlic, minced
1 C. canned artichoke hearts, drained
1/2 C. chopped red bell peppers
8 pitted Greek kalamata olives, chopped

1/2 t. dried oregano leaves
1/2 t. dried basil leaves
1/4 t. black pepper
3 T. grated Parmesan cheese, divided
1-16 oz. carton Egg Beaters

Spray a non-stick skillet with Pam. Heat over medium heat. Add the white portion of the green onions and garlic and cook 1 minute, stirring occasionally. Add the artichokes, bell peppers, olives, oregano, basil and black pepper. Cook 8 minutes. Remove and cover to keep warm. Pour the Egg Beaters into the same skillet. Cook until set in center, carefully pushing cooked eggs to center of skillet with a spatula and tilting skillet as necessary to allow uncooked portion to flow underneath. Spoon the vegetable mixture over half of the omelet and sprinkle with 2 tablespoons cheese. Fold omelet in half. Slide onto a serving plate. Top with remaining cheese and sprinkle with the green portion of the onions. Cut into 4 wedges. Serves 4.

Nutritional Information: 119 Calories, 3 g Fat, 8 g Carbohydrate, 4 mg Cholesterol, 397 mg Sodium, 14 g Protein, 2 g Fiber, 3 g Sugar,

Why limit "Happy" to an hour.

EGG AND GREEN CHILE CASSEROLE

1-8 oz. pkg. reduced-fat Monterey
  Jack cheese, shredded
1 C. reduced-fat Cheddar cheese,
  shredded
2-4 oz. cans chopped green chilies,
  drained

1 bunch green onions, chopped
5 eggs
7 egg whites
3 T. nonfat plain yogurt
1 tomato, thinly sliced

Do not preheat oven. Coat a 3-quart glass baking dish with non-stick cooking spray. Combine the first 4 ingredients. Spread on the bottom of the dish. Beat the eggs and egg whites together. Mix in the yogurt. Pour over the cheese mixture. Refrigerate overnight. Cook for 15 minutes in a 350 degrees F. oven. Add the sliced tomatoes along the top of the casserole and continue baking for 15 to 20 minutes longer. Serves 12.

Nutritional Information: 132 Calories, 7 g Fat, 3 g Carbohydrate, 104 mg Cholesterol, 312 mg Sodium, 13 g Protein, 1 g Fiber,

HAM AND EGG CASSEROLE

1 1/2 C. egg substitute
2 C. skim milk
1 C. reduced-fat sharp Cheddar
  cheese, shredded
1 t. mustard

3 slices whole wheat bread, torn
  into pieces
12 oz. turkey ham, cut into small
  pieces

Preheat oven to 350 degrees F. when ready to bake. Spray a 12x9x2-inch baking dish with a cooking spray. Cover the bottom of the dish with the bread. Spread the turkey ham over the bread. Combine the first 4 ingredients. Pour over the bread. Cover and refrigerate overnight. Bake for 45 minutes. Serves 8.

Nutritional Information: 161 Calories, 5 g Fat, 9 g Carbohydrate, 42 mg Cholesterol, 646 mg Sodium, 19 g Protein, 1 g Fiber,

HOME FRIES

8 oz. red potatoes, diced
1 onion, chopped

1/4 t. salt
Black pepper

Place the potatoes in the microwave and cook for 1 minute on high. Let rest. Repeat 2 more times. Place a non-stick skillet over medium-high heat. Spray lightly with the spray and add the diced onion. Cook, tossing frequently, until onion browns. Add the potatoes to the onions, salt and pepper. Spray lightly with oil and toss the fries until the potatoes are lightly browned. Serves 2.

Nutritional Information: 106 Calories, 0 g Fat, 24 g Carbohydrate, 0 mg Cholesterol, 299 mg Sodium, 3 g Fiber.

HASH BROWNED POTATOES

1 T. vegetable oil
2 baking potatoes, coarsely grated
1 onion, coarsely grated

1 garlic clove, minced
3/4 t. salt
1/4 t. black pepper

Warm the oil in a skillet over medium heat. In a bowl, add the rest of the ingredients and mix. Spread the potato mixture into the skillet. Top with a cake pan to weight down the potatoes. Cook 4 minutes. Turn and cook 4 more minutes. Serves 4.

Nutritional Information: 157 Calories, 4 g Fat, 29 g Carbohydrate, 0 mg Cholesterol, 409 mg Sodium, 3 g Protein, 1 g Fiber.

BLUEBERRY FRENCH TOAST

10 slices French bread, 1-inch
  thick
5 eggs, beaten
3/4 C. nonfat milk
1/3 C. lite silken tofu
1 t. vanilla extract

1/4 t. baking powder
24 oz. frozen blueberries
3/4 C. sugar
1 t. nutmeg
1 t. lemon zest

When ready to bake, preheat oven to 400 degrees F. Place bread slices in a 9x13-inch pan. In a blender, add the next 5 ingredients. Pour over the bread. Cover and refrigerate overnight. Remove from the refrigerator 30 minutes before baking. Remove the bread. Mix the rest of the ingredients and spread on the bottom of the pan. Cover with the bread. Bake 30 to 35 minutes. Serves 10.

Nutritional Information: 232 Calories, 4 g Fat, 43 g Carbohydrate, 106 mg Cholesterol, 8 g Protein, 3 g Fiber.

QUICK FRENCH TOAST

1 large egg
1/2 t. vanilla extract
1/4 t. cinnamon

1 pkg. artificial sweetener
1 T. skim milk
1 slice bread

Place all ingredients, except the bread, in a blender. Blend until combined. Pour egg mixture into a shallow bowl. Place the bread in the egg mixture and soak, turning once. Coat a non-stick skillet with a vegetable cooking spray and heat over medium heat. Place the bread in the skillet and pour any remaining egg mixture over the bread. Cook until browned on the bottom and then turn over to brown the other side. Serves 1.

Nutritional Information: 160 Calories, 6 g Fat, 14 g Carbohydrate, 215 mg Cholesterol, 200 mg Sodium, 9 gm Protein, 0 g Fiber.

FRENCH TOAST PUFF

1 C. egg substitute
1/2 C. evaporated skimmed milk
1 T. honey

1/2 t. cinnamon
4-1 oz. sliced cinnamon-raisin
   bread, cut diagonally in half

Spray a 9-inch pie plate with cooking spray. When ready to bake, preheat oven to 350 degrees F. In a bowl, add all the ingredients, except the bread. Place the bread in the prepared plate and pour the milk mixture over. Cover with plastic wrap and refrigerate at least 1 hour or overnight. Bake 25 to 30 minutes. Garnish with powdered sugar. Serves 4.

Nutritional Information: 141 Calories, 1 g Fat, 24 g Carbohydrate, 2 mg Cholesterol, 219 mg Sodium, 9 g Protein, 1 g Fiber.

BANANA WALNUT PANCAKES

1 C. flour
2 T. sugar
1 T. baking powder
1 C. fat-free milk

1 ripe banana, mashed
1/4 C. Egg Beaters
2 T. margarine, melted
1/2 C. chopped walnuts, toasted

Mix the first 3 ingredients. Mix in another bowl the remaining ingredients, except the walnuts. Mix the flour mixture with the egg mixture. Do not overmix. Batter should be slightly lumpy. Let stand 10 minutes. Stir in the walnuts. Spray a skillet with a cooking spray. Heat over medium-high. Pour the batter in the skillet, 1/4 cup at a time. Cook until bubbles form on top and then turn and cook 2 minutes. Repeat with remaining batter. Serve topped with more sliced bananas and cinnamon. Each serving is 3 pancakes.

Nutritional Information: 290 Calories, 11 g Fat, 40 g Carbohydrate, 1 mg Cholesterol, 478 mg Sodium, 9 g Protein, 3 g Fiber.

OATMEAL PANCAKES

1 1/2 C. dry oatmeal
2 C. low-fat buttermilk
2 egg whites

1 C. whole wheat flour
2 t. baking soda
1 banana, mashed

Combine the first 3 ingredients. Let stand for at least 1/2 hour. Add the remaining ingredients and mix well. Bake on a hot, lightly-oiled griddle. Each pancake should be 5 inches across. Makes 12 pancakes. Serving size is 1 pancake.

Nutritional Information: 98 Calories, 1 g Fat, 18 g Carbohydrate, 1 mg Cholesterol, 189 mg Sodium, 5 g Protein, 2 g Fiber.

OATMEAL MUFFINS

1 C. dry oatmeal
1 C. low-fat buttermilk
1/4 C. margarine, melted
1/4 C. egg substitute
1/2 C. brown sugar

3/4 C. flour
1/4 C. whole wheat flour
1/2 t. baking soda
1 t. salt

When ready to cook, preheat oven to 400 degrees F. Spray a 15-cup muffin pan. Combine the oatmeal and buttermilk. Soak for 1 hour in the refrigerator. Mix the next 3 ingredients together. In another bowl, add the remaining ingredients. Mix the egg substitute and wheat mixture together, alternate with the oatmeal mixture. Fill the muffin tin 2/3-full. Bake for 15 to 20 minutes. Makes 15 muffins.

Nutritional Information: 111 Calories, 3 g Fat, 17 g Carbohydrate, 0 mg Cholesterol, 230 mg Sodium, 3 g Protein, 1 g Fiber.

CRUNCHY BLUEBERRY MUFFINS

2 C. flour
1/2 C. sugar
1 t. baking powder
1/2 t. salt
1/2 t. cinnamon

1/2 C. cholesterol-free egg
    substitute
1 1/4 C. nonfat sour cream
1/4 C. Karo syrup
1 C. Grape-Nuts
1/2 C. blueberries

Preheat oven to 375 degrees F. Line muffin cups with paper liners. Blend the first 5 ingredients. In another bowl, whip the egg substitute until foamy. Add and blend the sour cream and syrup. Mix until blended. Fold in the blueberries and cereal. Pour into the muffin cups. Bake 25 to 30 minutes. Makes 12 muffins.

Nutritional Information: 186 Calories, 42 g Carbohydrate, 0 mg Cholesterol, 172 mg Sodium, 5 g Protein, 1 g Fiber.

BANANA BRAN MUFFINS

1 1/2 C. shredded wheat bran
    cereal
1 1/2 C. fat-free milk
1 1/2 C. flour
1/2 C. firmly-packed brown sugar

1 T. baking powder
1/2 C. Egg Beaters
1/4 C. margarine, melted
1 t. vanilla extract
1 C. mashed ripe bananas

Preheat oven to 400 degrees F. Spray 12 muffin cups with baking spray. Set aside. Stir together the cereal and milk and let stand 5 minutes. Combine the flour, sugar and baking powder. Set aside. Add the Egg Beaters, margarine and vanilla to the cereal mixture. Beat with a wire whisk until well blended. Stir in the flour mixture and bananas just until combined. Spoon into the muffin cups. Bake 20 minutes. Makes 12 servings.

Nutritional Information: 176 Calories, 5 g Fat, 32 g Carbohydrate, 1 mg Cholesterol, 206 mg Sodium, 5 g Protein, 4 g Fiber.

BANANA BREAD

1 1/2 C. mashed bananas
2 egg whites
1 C. sugar
1 t. vanilla extract
1/4 C. canola oil

1/2 C. plain nonfat yogurt
2 1/4 C. flour
1/4 t. salt
1 1/2 t. baking powder
1/2 t. baking soda

Preheat oven to 375 degrees F. Coat a loaf pan with non-stick spray. With an electric mixer on medium speed, beat the first 6 ingredients. In another bowl, mix the rest of the ingredients. At low speed, add the dry ingredients a little at a time with the banana mixture. Pour in the loaf pan and bake 50 to 60 minutes, until center tests clean. Cool in pan 10 minutes. Serves 12.

Nutritional Information: 210 Calories, 5 g Fat, 40 g Carbohydrate, 0 mg Cholesterol, 140 mg Sodium, 4 gm Protein, 1 g Fiber, 23 g Sugar,

GRANOLA

4 C. old-fashioned oatmeal
1/2 C. wheat bran
2 T. nonfat dry milk
1 t. ground cinnamon
1/2 C. sunflower seeds

1/2 C. pumpkin seeds
2/3 C. honey
2 T. molasses
1/2 C. dried cranberries
1 C. dried mixed fruit bits

Preheat oven to 300 degrees F. Line a baking sheet with heavy foil. Mix the first 6 ingredients. Spread in the pan. In a small bowl, mix together the honey and molasses. Pour over the cereal, stirring until well coated. Bake for 30 to 35 minutes, mixing every 15 minutes. Let cool and toss with remaining ingredients. Store in airtight container. 16 (1/2-cup) servings.

Nutritional Information: 214 Calories, 6 g Fat, 38 g Carbohydrate, 0 mg Cholesterol, 10 gm Sodium, 6 g Protein, 4 g Fiber.

BLUEBERRY YOGURT CRUNCH

1-8 oz. nonfat sweetened vanilla
  yogurt

1/2 C. blueberries
1/4 C. bran cereal

Combine all ingredients. Serves 1.

Nutritional Information: 190 Calories, 1 g Fat, 44 g Carbohydrate, 5 mg Cholesterol, 250 mg Sodium, 8 g Protein, 11 g Fiber.

STRAWBERRY-PAPAYA SHAKE

1/2 of a papaya, peeled, seeded
  and chopped
1/2 C. fresh strawberries
1/2 C. fat-free milk

1/2 C. plain fat-free yogurt
1 T. honey
3 large ice cubes

In a blender, combine all the ingredients, except the ice cubes. Cover and blend until smooth. With the blender running, add the ice cubes, one at a time. Serves 2.

Nutritional Information: 117 Calories, 0 gm Fat, 24 g Carbohydrate, 2 mg Cholesterol, 78 mg Sodium, 6 gm Protein, 1 g Fiber.

HOT FRUIT CASSEROLE

1-20 oz. can pineapple chunks in
   their own juice
2-16 oz. pkg. frozen sliced peaches
1-16 oz. can pitted tart red cherries,
   drained
4 bananas, peeled and sliced

2 T. lemon juice
2/3 C. light brown sugar
1 C. vanilla wafer crumbs
4 T. margarine, cut up
1/3 C. crème de banana liqueur

Preheat oven to 350 degrees F. In a bowl, mix the first 3 ingredients. Sprinkle the bananas with the lemon juice and add to the other fruit. Place half of the fruit mixture in a 3-quart casserole dish. Sprinkle with half the brown sugar, half the vanilla wafer crumbs, half the margarine and half the crème de banana. Repeat with the remaining ingredients. Bake 35 to 45 minutes. Serve hot. Makes 10 servings.

Nutritional Information: 258 Calories, 6 g Fat, 49 g Carbohydrate, 1 mg Cholesterol, 86 mg Sodium, 3 g Protein, 3 g Fiber.

MEXICAN SALSA BREAD

1 C. shredded reduced-fat
   Monterey Jack cheese, divided
3/4 C. picante sauce

1/3 C. chipped fresh cilantro
1 lb. Italian cheese-flavored pizza
   crust

Preheat oven to 350 degrees F. Combine 1/2 cup cheese, picante sauce and cilantro in a bowl and mix well. Spoon over the pizza crust and sprinkle with remaining cheese. Place on a baking sheet and bake for 15 minutes. Cut into wedges. Serving size is 1 wedge.

Nutritional Information: 143 Calories, 4.9 g Fat, 1.3 g Carbohydrate, 13 mg Cholesterol, 520 mg Sodium, 8.9 g Protein, 0.1 g Fiber.

TEX-MEX CORNBREAD

1 C. yellow cornmeal
1 C. flour
2 t. baking powder
2 t. chili powder
1 t. ground cumin
1/2 t. baking soda
1/8 t. cayenne pepper

1 C. fat-free milk
1 T. + 1 t. vegetable oil
2 T. honey
3/4 C. frozen no-salt-added whole
  kernel corn, thawed
1 jalapeño, seeded and chopped

Preheat oven to 400 degrees F. Lightly spray an 8-inch baking pan with vegetable oil spray. Set aside. Combine the first 7 ingredients. Make a well in the center. In another bowl, whisk together the milk, oil and honey. Pour into the well of the cornbread mixture. Whisk just until blended. Stir in the corn and jalapeños. Pour into the pan. Bake 20 to 25 minutes. Serves 8.

Nutritional Information: 92 Calories, 1.5 g Fat, 18 g Carbohydrate, 0 mg Cholesterol, 112 mg Sodium, 2 g Protein, 1 g Fiber.

Remember, as far as anyone knows, we're a nice, normal family.

NOTES & RECIPES

APPETIZERS

NOTES

VIDALIA SWEET ONION DIP

1 C. mayonnaise
2 C. shredded Swiss cheese
1/2 C. grated Parmesan cheese

2 C. thinly-sliced Vidalia sweet
  onion
Hot sauce, to taste

Preheat oven to 350 degrees F. Stir in all the ingredients and put in a casserole dish. Bake in the oven until the edges are golden brown, 30 to 35 minutes. Allow to cool 10 minutes before serving. Serves 44.

Nutritional Information: 61 Calories, 5.6 g Fat, 0.9 g Carbohydrate, 7 mg Cholesterol, 53 mg Sodium, 1.8 g Protein.

SHRIMP TACO DIP

8 oz. less-fat cream cheese
2 T. low-fat milk
1/2 C. chili sauce
1 C. fresh or frozen tiny shrimp,
  drained, rinsed

4 scallions, chopped
3/4 C. chopped green bell pepper
1 C. grated part-skim Mozzarella
  cheese

Mix the cream cheese and milk in a mixing bowl until smooth. Spread on a small serving platter. Layer the ingredients on top of the cream cheese, in the order that they appear on the list. Chill at least 1 hour before serving. Serve with reduced-fat tortilla chips. Serves 8.

Nutritional Information: 154 Calories, 8 g Fat, 8 g Carbohydrate, 55 mg Cholesterol, 560 mg Sodium, 11 g Protein, 1 g Fiber.

SPINACH ARTICHOKE HEART DIP

1 T. minced garlic
1/4 C. chopped green onions
1-10 oz. pkg. frozen chopped
  spinach, thawed and squeezed of
  excess water
1-14 oz. can artichoke hearts,
  drained and chopped
1 T. whipped butter, melted

2 C. fat-free half and half
4 T. flour
1/8 t. ground nutmeg
1/8 t. white pepper
4 T. shredded Parmesan cheese
1 C. shredded part-skim
  Mozzarella cheese
1/3 T. grated Parmesan cheese

Preheat the oven to 350 degrees F. Coat the inside of slow cooker with canola cooking spray. In a non-stick pan, melt the butter. Stir in 1/3 cup of the half and half, flour, nutmeg and pepper. Slowly stir in the remaining half and half. Bring the mixture to a gently boil over medium-high heat. Reduce heat to medium-low and continue to gently boil, stirring constantly, until sauce thickens, about 4 minutes. Stir in the 4 tablespoons Parmesan cheese. Add this and the rest of the ingredients and mix. Add to slow cooker and heat on high for 60 minutes. Makes 16 servings.

Nutritional Information: 75 Calories, 3.5 g Fat, 5 g Carbohydrate, 11 mg Cholesterol, 150 mg Sodium, 6 g Protein, 2 g Fiber.

The only green vegetables I get are olives.

CREAMY SEAFOOD DIP

4 oz. light cream cheese, room
  temperature
1 pt. low-fat cottage cheese
3 T. lemon juice
2 t. prepared horseradish

1/4 t. Tabasco sauce
1/4 C. chopped green onion
1-6 1/2 oz. can minced shrimp,
  drained

In a blender, add the first 5 ingredients, and blend until smooth. Stir in the onions and seafood. Makes 24 servings. Two tablespoons makes 1 serving.

Nutritional Information: 30 Calories, 1 g Fat.

AVOCADO DIP

1/2 C. fat-free sour cream
2 T. chopped onion
1/2 C. salsa

1/8 t. hot sauce
1 ripe avocado, peeled, pitted and
  mashed

Mix all ingredients. Serving size 1/4 cup.

Nutritional Information: 64 Calories, 5 g Total Fat, 1 g Saturated Fat, 4 g Carbohydrate, 0 mg Cholesterol, 27 mg Sodium, 2 g Protein, 2 g Fiber.

BLACK BEAN DIP

1-19 oz. black beans, rinsed
1/2 C. prepared salsa
2 T. fresh lime juice

2 T. chopped fresh cilantro
1/4 t. ground cumin
Salt and pepper, to taste

Combine all the ingredients in a food processor and process until smooth. Cover and refrigerate. Makes 1 1/2 cups. Serving size 1 tablespoon.

Nutritional Information: 17 Calories, 0 g Fat, 3 g Carbohydrate, 0 mg Cholesterol, 65 mg Sodium, 1 g Protein, 1 g Fiber, 2 mg potassium.

EGGPLANT DIP

1 lb. eggplant
1/3 C. golden raisins, chopped
2 T. water
2 T. chopped fresh basil
2 t. fresh lemon juice
1 t. olive oil
1/4 t. black pepper

1/8 t. salt
1 garlic clove, minced
4-6-inch pitas
1/2 C. shredded part-skim
   Mozzarella cheese
3 T. grated Parmesan cheese

Preheat oven to 425 degrees F. Pierce eggplant several times with a fork and wrap in foil. Place the eggplant on a baking sheet and bake for 1 hour. Cool slightly. Peel, seed and mash eggplant with a potato masher. Add the raisins and water in a bowl. Cover with plastic wrap and vent. Microwave at high 30 seconds. Let stand covered for 10 minutes and then drain. Add the rest of the ingredients to the garlic. Mix well. Preheat broiler. Sprinkle the pitas with the cheeses and broil for 2 minutes, or until cheese melts. Cut each pita into 6 wedges and serve with the eggplant dip.

Nutritional Information: 48 Calories, 1 g Fat, 8 g Carbohydrate, 2 mg Cholesterol, 41 mg Sodium, 2 g Protein, 1 g Fiber, 43 mg Calcium.

SPINACH DIP

1 medium whole head garlic
1 t. olive oil
1-10 oz. pkg. frozen chopped
  spinach
1/4 C. fat-free milk
1/8 t. salt

Dash of bottled hot pepper sauce
1-8 oz. pkg. reduced-fat cream
  cheese
Chopped tomato
Toasted pita wedges

Preheat oven to 375 degrees F. Peel away outer dry leaves from head of garlic, leaving skin of garlic cloves intact. Cut off the top portion of the garlic head, leaving the bulb intact. Place garlic head on a 12-inch square of a double thickness of foil. Drizzle garlic with the oil. Fold the foil to enclose the garlic. Bake for 30 minutes. Cool. Cook the spinach according to the package directions. Drain well, pressing out excess liquid. Squeeze the garlic pulp from each clove into a food processor bowl, discarding the skins. Add the spinach, milk, salt and hot pepper sauce. Cover and process. Add cream cheese. Cover and process until nearly smooth. Place mixture into a saucepan. Cook and stir over medium-low heat until heated through. Transfer to a serving bowl. Sprinkle with the chopped tomato. Serve with the pita wedges. Makes 8-1/4-cup servings.

Nutritional Information: 133 Calories, 7 g Fat, 12 gm Carbohydrate, 22 mg Cholesterol, 246 mg Sodium, 5 g Protein, 0 g Fiber.

Three wise men,
Are you serious?

PARMESAN ARTICHOKE DIP

4 oz. light cream cheese
1/2 C. light mayonnaise
1 1/2 t. minced garlic
3/4 C. shredded Parmesan cheese
14 oz. can artichoke hearts,
  drained and chopped

2 T. dry white wine
1/4 C. finely-chopped red bell
  pepper
2 T. chopped can green chilies

Preheat oven to 350 degrees F. Add the cream cheese, mayonnaise and garlic in a bowl and beat on medium-low until blended. Add the remaining ingredients and mix well. Spoon mixture into a 1 1/2-quart casserole and bake for 30 minutes. Serves 6.

Nutritional Information: 164 Calories, 10 g Fat, 11 gm Carbohydrate, 13 mg Cholesterol, 353 mg Sodium, 6 g Protein, 4 g Fiber.

I don't have hot flashes. I have short private vacations in the tropics.

7 LAYER DIP

1 avocado, peeled, pitted and
  diced
2 t. lime juice
2 T. chopped fresh cilantro
2 T. salsa
Garlic powder
Salt and pepper, to taste
8 oz. fat-free sour cream

1 oz. pkg. taco seasoning mix
15 oz. can fat-free refried beans
1 C. diced tomatoes, drained
1/2 C. finely-chopped green
  onions
2 C. shredded reduced-fat
  Mexican-style cheese blend
2 1/4 oz. can sliced black beans

Mix the first 6 ingredients. Set aside. In a bowl, blend the sour cream with the taco seasoning. Spread the beans in the bottom of a deep-dish pie plate. Top the beans with the sour cream mixture. Top with the avocado mixture. Spread the tomatoes on top, then sprinkle the green onions over the top. Sprinkle the cheese and olives on the top. Serve with reduced-fat tortilla chips. Makes 16 servings.

Nutritional Information: 85 Calories, 4.4 g Fat, 6.4 g Carbohydrate, 7 mg Cholesterol, 258 mg Sodium, 5.2 g Protein, 0.7 g Fiber.

Does wine count as a serving of fruit?

HUMMUS

1-19-oz. can chickpeas, rinsed and
  drained
1/2 C. fresh lemon juice
1/2 C. tahini
2 cloves garlic, minced
1 t. vegetable oil
1/2 t. ground cumin

1/8 t. cayenne pepper
Fresh-ground black pepper, to
  taste
1/4 t. salt
1/4 C. water
1/2 C. finely-chopped fresh
  parsley

In a food processor, combine all the ingredients, except the parsley and blend until smooth. Stir in the parsley. Cover and refrigerate for 24 hours.

Nutritional Information: 176 Calories, 7 g Fat, 22 gm Carbohydrate, 0 mg Cholesterol, 9 g Protein.

QUICK GUACAMOLE

Kendall Saba, Chandler, AZ

1 medium ripe avocado, peeled
  and cubed
1 T. salsa

1 garlic clove, peeled
1/4 t. salt

Combine all the ingredients in a food processor. Process until smooth. Serves 6.

Nutritional Information: 53 Calories, 5 g Fat, 2 gm Carbohydrate, 0 mg Cholesterol, 114 mg Sodium, 1 g Protein, 2 g Fiber.

CRANBERRY SALSA

4 oz. 100% cranberry juice blend
1 1/2 C. diced tomatoes
1 C. fresh cranberries, sliced thin
1/4 C. ripe avocado, diced
1/2 C. pineapple, diced
1/2 C. scallions, sliced thinly

2 T. lemon juice
1/4 C. jalapeño peppers, chopped fine
2 cloves crushed garlic
Fresh ground pepper

Place the juice in a saucepan. Boil for about 5 minutes until reduced to about 1 tablespoon of syrup. Place the juice and rest of the ingredients into a bowl and stir. Chill. Makes 8 servings.

Nutritional Information: 40 Calories, 0 g Fat, 8 g Carbohydrate, 0 mg Cholesterol, 76 mg Sodium, 0 g Protein, 1 g Fiber.

MANGO PAPAYA SALSA

1 mango, peeled, seeded and diced
1 papaya, peeled, seeded and diced
1 red pepper, seeded and diced
1 avocado, peeled, pitted and diced

1/2 C. sweet onion, peeled and finely diced
2 T. fresh chopped fresh cilantro
2 T. balsamic vinegar
Salt and pepper, to taste

Add all the ingredients. Cover and chill in the refrigerator at least 30 minutes. Serve with reduced-fat tortilla chips. Serves 6.

Nutritional Information: 84 Calories, 4 g Fat, 12.6 g Carbohydrate, 0 mg Cholesterol, 5 mg Sodium, 1 g Protein, 3 g Fiber.

RED AND GREEN BELL PEPPER BOATS

Grace Qualls, Lafayette, LA

1 medium green bell pepper
1 medium red bell pepper
1/4 C. sliced almonds
4 oz. low-fat cream cheese,
  softened

1 t. salt-free lemon pepper
  seasoning blend
1 t. fresh lemon juice

Cut each bell pepper in half lengthwise, discard the stems, ribs and seeds. Cut each half into six pieces. Arrange the pieces with the skin side down on a platter. Set aside. In a skillet, dry-roast the almonds over medium heat for 3 to 4 minutes. Transfer 1 tablespoon of the almonds to a plate and reserve for garnish. Process the remaining almonds in a food processor for 15 to 20 seconds. In a mixing bowl, beat the cream cheese, lemon pepper seasoning blend and lemon juice with a mixer until creamy. Add the ground almonds and beat for 10 seconds. Spoon onto the peppers and garnish with the sliced almonds.

Nutritional Information: 57 Calories, 4 g Fat, 3 g Carbohydrate, 8 mg Cholesterol, 43 mg Sodium, 2 g Protein, 1 g Fiber.

Dinner will be ready when the smoke alarm goes off.

SPINACH SQUARES

1 egg
1/4 C. egg substitute
1/2 C. low-fat milk
1 C. flour
1 t. salt
1 t. baking powder

2 T. canola margarine, melted
1/3 C. fat-free sour cream
8 oz. reduced-fat Monterey Jack
   cheese, cut into 1/2-inch cubes
2-10 oz. boxes frozen chopped
   spinach, thawed and drained

Preheat oven to 325 degrees F. Coat a 9x9-inch baking dish with canola cooking spray. Beat the first 7 ingredients with a hand mixer until smooth. Stir in the cheese cubes and spinach. Pour into the pan and bake 35 minutes. Let sit about 10 minutes before serving. Cut the spinach into squares after they come out of the oven. Makes 9 servings.

Nutritional Information: 188 Calories, 8 g Fat, 17 g Carbohydrate, 45 mg Cholesterol, 525 mg Sodium, 12.5 g Protein, 2 g Fiber.

If I keel over at Wal-Mart, drag my body to Neiman's!

SPINACH PINWHEELS

1 T. + 2 t. olive oil
1/2 C. chopped onion
4 garlic cloves, chopped
2 C. thawed and well drained
  frozen chopped spinach
2 T. chopped fresh parsley

1/8 t. crushed pepper
1/3 C. grated Parmesan cheese
1-10 oz. pkg. refrigerated ready to
  bake pizza crust dough
1 T. thawed frozen egg substitute

Preheat oven to 425 degrees F. Heat the oil in a skillet. Add the onion and garlic and cook over medium-high heat, stirring frequently, until onion softens, about 3 minutes. Add the spinach, parsley and red pepper and cook, stirring occasionally, until spinach is heated through about 3 minutes. Let cool slightly and add the cheese and stir. Stretch pizza dough into a 16x12-inch rectangle. Spread spinach mixture evenly over the dough, leaving a 1 1/2-inch border around the edge of the dough. Starting from the narrow end roll dough over spinach, jellyroll fashion, to enclose filling. Pinch the seam well to seal. Spray a non-stick baking sheet with non-stick cooking spray and arrange roll, seam side down, on the sheet. Brush egg substitute over the roll and bake until golden brown, about 15 minutes. Cut roll into 20 equal slices.

Nutritional Information: 120 Calories, 4 g Fat, 16 g Carbohydrate, 2 mg Cholesterol, 219 mg Sodium, 5 g Protein, 88 mg Calcium.

Discover wildlife-teach school.

PESTO PINWHEELS

1-8 oz. can refrigerated crescent
  rolls
1/3 C. prepared pesto sauce

1/4 C. roasted sweet red peppers,
  drained and chopped
1/4 C. grated Parmesan cheese
1 C. pizza sauce, warmed

Preheat oven to 400 degrees F. Unroll crescent dough into two long rectangles, seal seams and perforations. Spread each with pesto, sprinkle with red peppers and cheese. Roll each up jellyroll style, starting with a short side. With a knife, cut each roll into 10 slices. Place cut-side down, 2 inches apart, on 2 ungreased baking sheets. Bake for 8 to 10 minutes. Serve warm with pizza sauce. 20 servings.

Nutritional Information: 76 Calories, 5 g Fat, 1 g Saturated Fat, 6 g Carbohydrate, 2 mg Cholesterol, 201 mg Sodium, 2 g Protein, 0 g Fiber.

Who needs a spring chicken when you have a well seasoned bird.

CHICKEN PICADILLO NACHOS

1/2 t. vegetable oil
8 oz. ground chicken or turkey
1/2 t. ground cumin
1/2 t. dried oregano
1/2 t. salt
2 jalapeño peppers, seeded and
   finely chopped
1 t. flour
1 t. chili powder
3 T. raisins

1 T. cider vinegar
2 t. sugar
1-14.5-oz. can diced tomatoes,
   drained
1-16 oz. can pink beans, drained
40 baked tortilla chips
1/2 C. bottled salsa
1/2 C. shredded sharp Cheddar
   cheese

Preheat oven to 450° degrees F. Heat oil in a large non-stick skillet over medium-high heat. Add the chicken, cumin, oregano, salt and jalapeños. Cook until chicken is browned, stirring to crumble. Stir in the flour and chili powder, cooking 1 minute. Add the raisins, vinegar, sugar and tomatoes. Cook 3 minutes, stirring frequently. Add the beans. Cook until thoroughly heated. Arrange the chips on a large baking sheet. Spoon the chicken mixture and salsa evenly over the chips. Sprinkle with the cheese. Bake for 5 minutes or until cheese is melted.

Nutritional Information: 208 Calories, 6 g Fat, 28 g Carbohydrate, 31 mg Cholesterol, 545 mg Sodium, 12 g Protein, 4 g Fiber, 123 mg calcium.

Life's uncertain. Eat dessert first.

CRAB-STUFFED MUSHROOMS

3 T. light mayonnaise
3 T. fat-free sour cream
3 T. Italian seasoned dry bread
  crumbs
3 T. shredded Parmesan cheese
1 t. finely-chopped garlic

1-6 1/2 oz. can crabmeat
Dash of Tabasco sauce
Black pepper, to taste
18 medium sized mushrooms,
  washed and stems removed

Preheat a slow-cooker to high heat. In a small bowl, add the first 5 ingredients. Fold in the crabmeat. Add the Tabasco and black pepper. Spoon heaping teaspoonful of the crab filling into the mushrooms caps. Arrange the caps, crab-side up, in the bottom of the slow-cooker. Add, cover and cook for 2 hours. Reduce heat to low and serve the mushrooms. Makes 9 servings. Two mushrooms per serving.

Nutritional Information: 59 Calories, 2.5 g Fat, 0.6 g Saturated Fat, 4 g Carbohydrate, 16 mg Cholesterol, 177 mg Sodium, 5 g Protein, 0.5 g Fiber.

CRAB-STUFFED DEVILED EGGS

6 large eggs, hard-cooked eggs,
  cooled and peeled
1/4 C. clean and shredded crab
2 T. finely-chopped red pepper
2 T. finely-chopped green onion

2 T. light mayonnaise
2 t. Dijon mustard
Dash of ground nutmeg
1/2 t. parsley flakes
Black pepper, to taste

Cut eggs in half lengthwise and remove the yolks. Place half of the yolks in a bowl and mash with a fork. You can throw the other half away. Add the rest of the ingredients and blend with a fork. Spoon mixture among the 12 egg white halves. Makes 6 servings. Two eggs, per serving.

Nutritional Information: 70 Calories, 4.5 g Fat, 1 g Saturated Fat, 1 g Carbohydrate, 111 mg Cholesterol, 151 mg Sodium, 6 g Protein, 0.1 g Fiber.

SAUSAGE BALLS

12 oz. pkg. Jimmy Dean light
  sausage
8 oz. pkg. shredded reduced-fat
  sharp Cheddar cheese

2 C. reduced-fat Bisquick
1/4 C. low-fat milk

Preheat oven to 400 degrees F. Coat a non-stick jellyroll pan with canola cooking spray. Add all the ingredients and mix well. Roll into 1-inch balls (about 60) and place on the pan. Coat the tops of the sausage balls with the cooking spray. Bake for about 15 minutes. Makes 60 balls. Serving size 5 balls.

Nutritional Information: 175 Calories, 8 g Fat, 3 g Saturated Fat, 15 g Carbohydrate, 35 mg Cholesterol, 498 mg Sodium, 11 g Protein, 0.3 g Fiber.

TEXAS CHEESE BALL

2 C. shredded Cheddar cheese
1-8 oz. pkg. reduced-fat cream
  cheese
2 T. reduced-fat butter
1/8 t. onion powder
1/8 t. garlic powder

1/4 C. chopped green chilies
1/2 C. baked nacho tortilla chips,
  crushed
1 T. minced fresh cilantro
Tortilla chips

In a food processor, combine the first 5 ingredients. Cover and process until blended. Stir in the chilies. Cover and refrigerate for 1 hour. Shape into a ball. Combine crushed tortilla chips and cilantro. Roll the cheese basil in the chip mixture. Makes 2 cups. Two tablespoons serving size.

Nutritional Information: 94 Calories, 8 g Fat, 5 g Saturated Fat, 2 g Carbohydrate, 27 mg Cholesterol, 169 mg Sodium, 5 g Protein, 0 g Fiber.

PIZZA PUFFS

1-10 oz. can refrigerated pizza
  dough
1/4 C. pizza sauce

1 C. grated part-skim Mozzarella
  cheese
12 to 14 slices pepperoni

Preheat oven to 375 degrees F. Roll out the pizza dough on a lightly-floured surface to 1/8-inch thickness. Using a round cookie cutter cut circles of dough. Place 1/2 teaspoon of the pizza sauce in the center of each circle. Do not spread. top with a slice of the pepperoni and 1 teaspoon of cheese. Wrap dough around the filling and pinch shut. Place seam-side down on a greased cookie sheet. Brush tops lightly with water. Bake for 15 to 17 minutes, until lightly browned. Makes 12 to 14 puffs, serving size 1 puff.

Nutritional Information: 98 Calories, 4 g Fat, 9 g Carbohydrate, 8 mg Cholesterol, 284 mg Sodium, 5 g Protein, 1 g Fiber.

CRANBERRY CREAM CHEESE

Alexa Saba, Chandler, AZ

2/3 C. light cream cheese

1/3 C. cranberry sauce

Mix the 2 ingredients with a mixer on low speed. Cover and refrigerate. Makes 16 tablespoons, serving size 1 tablespoon. Serve with crackers.

Nutritional Information: 32 Calories, 1.7 g Fat, 3 g Carbohydrate, 5 mg Cholesterol, 51 mg Sodium, 1 g Protein, 1 g Fiber.

TOMATO BRUSCHETTA

3 fresh, ripe roma tomatoes,
  chopped in small pieces
4 basil leaves, chopped in small
  pieces
1 t. fresh oregano leaves, chopped
  in small pieces

1 t. minced garlic
4 slices French bread, about 1/2-
  inch thick
1 1/2 T. extra-virgin olive oil
Salt and pepper, to taste

Mix the first 4 ingredients together. Toast the bread slices. Spoon the
tomato mixture on the bread. Sprinkle with the salt and pepper. Drizzle
1 teaspoon of olive oil on top of each. Serves 4.

Nutritional Information: 146 Calories, 6.4 g Fat, 19.5 g Carbohydrate, 0
mg Cholesterol, 181 mg Sodium, 3.5 g Protein, 1.5 g Fiber.

SEAFOOD BRUSCHETTA

3 T. olive oil
1 T. lemon juice
1 T. snipped fresh chives
1 T. snipped fresh basil
1 T. snipped fresh mint
1 t. bottled minced garlic
6 oz. frozen crabmeat, thawed and
  drained

8 oz. peeled, deveined, cooked
  shrimp, coarsely chopped
1 C. chopped plum tomatoes
1/2 C. finely-chopped onion
1-8 oz. loaf baguette-style French
  bread
2 T. olive oil
Ground black pepper

Add all the ingredients, except the bread, and toss to coat. Cut the bread
into 48 thin slices. Brush each side with 2 tablespoons olive oil. Sprinkle
lightly with the pepper. Broil the bread on both sides. To serve, spoon
seafood mixture onto the bread. Makes 48 servings.

Nutritional Information: 32 Calories, 1 g total Fat, 3 g Carbohydrate, 13
mg Cholesterol, 48 mg Sodium, 2 g Protein, 0 g Fiber.

SOUPS
AND
SALADS

NOTES

BARLEY AND VEGETABLE SOUP

1 t. vegetable oil
1/2 C. pearl barley
3 medium fresh mushrooms, chopped
6 C. fat-free, no-salt-added beef broth
1 medium potato, peeled and diced
2 medium carrots, peeled and sliced
2 medium leeks, white part only, finely chopped
1 rib of celery, sliced
1 t. dried marjoram
1/2 t. dried mustard
1/4 t. ground allspice
1/8 t. pepper
1/3 C. nonfat sour cream
1/4 C. snipped fresh parsley

Heat the oil over medium heat in a stockpot. Cook the barley and mushrooms for 1 to 2 minutes. Add the broth. Increase the heat to high and bring the mixture to a boil. Reduce the heat and simmer, covered, for 15 minutes, stirring occasionally. Add the potato, carrots, leeks and celery to the barley mixture. Stir in the thyme, marjoram, mustard, allspice and pepper. Simmer, covered, for 30 minutes. Top each serving with 2 teaspoons sour cream and a sprinkling of parsley. Serves 8.

Nutritional Information: 105 Calories, 1 g Fat, 19 g Carbohydrate, 0 mg Cholesterol, 79 mg Sodium, 7 gm Protein, 3 g Fiber.

It's not burnt, it's blackened.

CORN AND GREEN CHILI CHOWDER

1 C. water
4 potatoes, diced
1 can diced green chilies
1/2 C. diced celery
1/2 C. diced onion
2 1/2 t. chicken bouillon granules
1 t. Mrs. Dash

1/4 t. ground white pepper
4 C. fresh, frozen or canned corn
3 C. skim milk
1/4 C. + 2 T. instant nonfat milk
   powder
3 T. finely-chopped chives

Combine the first 7 ingredients. Bring to a boil, reduce heat to low, cover and simmer for 15 minutes. Add the corn and simmer for 5 more minutes. Combine the milk and milk powder in a bowl. Add the milk mixture to the pot and cook, stirring constantly, about 5 minutes. Blend soup in a blender at low speed, 2 to 3 cups at a time. Simmer the soup in the pot for 5 more minutes. Garnish with the chives. Serves 4.

Nutritional Information: 164 Calories, 1.1 g Fat, 2 mg Cholesterol, 360 mg Sodium, 7.8 g Protein, 3.1 g Fiber.

Skinny cooks can't be trusted.

COUNTRY CHICKEN GUMBO

1/3 C. flour
3 C. nonfat chicken broth
2 skinless, boneless chicken
  breasts
1-10 oz. pkg. frozen cut okra,
  thawed
1/2 C. chopped onions

1/3 C. chopped celery
4 cloves garlic, minced
1/4 t. ground black pepper
1/4 t. ground red pepper
2 bay leaves
2 C. hot cooked rice

Lightly spray a skillet with non-stick spray. Heat the skillet over medium heat. Add the flour. Cook and stir until the flour turns reddish brown. Slowly stir in the broth. Then add the chicken, okra, onions, celery, garlic, black pepper, red pepper and bay leaves. Bring to a boil, then reduce the heat. Cover and simmer for 20 to 30 minutes. Remove and discard the bay leaves. Serve over the rice. Serves 4.

Nutritional Information: 161 Calories, 1 g Fat, 35 mg Cholesterol.

I take life with a grain of salt, a wedge of lime and a shot of tequila.

NEW ENGLAND CLAM CHOWDER

2-6 1/2 oz. cans minced clams with the juice, drained and juices saved
2 1/2 C. peeled and finely-chopped potatoes
1 C. chopped onions
1 t. instant chicken bouillon granules

1 t. Worcestershire sauce
1/4 t. dried thyme
1/8 t. ground black pepper
1 1/2 C. 1% milk
3 T. cornstarch
1 1/2 C. evaporated skim milk
1/4 t. liquid smoke

Make 1 cup from the clam juice, adding water if needed. In a medium saucepan, combine the juice, potatoes, onions, granules, Worcestershire sauce, thyme and black pepper. Bring to a boil, then reduce the heat. Cover and simmer about 5 minutes. Using the back of a fork, slightly mash the potatoes against the side of the pan. In a small bowl, stir together the 1% milk and cornstarch. Add to the potato mixture. Mix in the rest of the ingredients to the potato mixture. Cook for 1 minute, stirring frequently. Serves 4.

Nutritional Information: 259 Calories, 2 gm Fat, 40 mg Cholesterol.

Alcohol is the answer. I don't remember the question.

BLACK BEAN AND CORN SALAD

1-15 oz. can black beans, rinsed
   and drained
2 C. fresh or thawed frozen corn
2 jalapeño chili peppers, seeded
   and finely chopped
2 plum tomatoes, chopped
1/2 C. red onion, finely chopped

2 garlic cloves, minced
1/4 C. chopped fresh cilantro
2 T. lime juice
1 T. olive oil
2 t. southwest-style seasoning mix
1/4 t. salt

Combine the first 7 ingredients. Toss well. Mix the rest of the ingredients and pour over the salad. Cover and refrigerate 1 hour before serving. Serves 4.

Nutritional Information: 183 Calories, 4 g Fat, 37 g Carbohydrate, 768 mg Sodium, 8 g Protein, 8 g Fiber.

BLACK BEAN SALAD

1-15 oz. can black beans, rinsed
   and drained
2-15 oz. cans whole kernel corn,
   drained
8 green onions, chopped
2 jalapeño peppers, seeded and
   minced
1 green bell pepper, chopped

1 avocado, peeled, pitted and
   diced
1-4 oz. jar pimentos
3 tomatoes, seeded and chopped
1 C. chopped fresh cilantro
1 lime, juiced
1/2 C. Italian salad dressing
1/2 t. garlic salt

Combine all the ingredients and mix well. Chill. Serves 12.

Nutritional Information: 178 Calories, 8.5 g Fat, 24.3 g Carbohydrate, 0 mg Cholesterol, 420 mg Sodium, 5 g Protein, 5.5 g Fiber.

CAESAR SALAD

2 T. extra-virgin olive oil
2 T. chicken broth
1 T. fat-free plain yogurt
1/2 t. lemon juice
1/2 t. Worcestershire sauce
1 t. anchovy paste

1 garlic clove, minced
1/4 t. ground black pepper
1/8 t. hot pepper sauce
1 head romaine lettuce, torn
3 T. grated Parmesan cheese
1/2 C. plain croutons

In a large bowl, mix the first 9 ingredients. Add the lettuce, cheese and croutons. Toss to coat. Serves 4.

Nutritional Information: 125 Calories, 9 g Fat, 7 g Carbohydrate, 4 mg Cholesterol, 208 mg Sodium, 5 g Protein, 2 g Fiber.

CHICKPEA SALAD

1-15 oz. can chickpeas (garbanzo beans), drained
1/2 onion, chopped
1/2 cucumber, sliced

1 tomato, chopped
1/2 C. red wine vinegar
1/2 C. balsamic vinegar

In a medium bowl, combine the first 4 ingredients. Mix the vinegars and pour over the salad. Mix well. Serves 4.

Nutritional Information: 171 Calories, 1.4 g Fat, 34.8 g Carbohydrate, 0 mg Cholesterol, 5.9 g Protein, 5.4 g Fiber.

SUMMER CORN SALAD

1-15.25 oz. can whole kernel corn, drained
1-15.25 oz. can white corn, drained
2 tomatoes, chopped
1/2-15 oz. can sweet peas, drained
1 cucumber, diced
1 purple onion, diced
3 T. pimentos
1 C. mayonnaise
Salt and pepper, to taste

Add all ingredients and mix. Cover and chill 1 hour. Serves 12.

Nutritional Information: 209 Calories, 15.4 g Fat, 17.8 g Carbohydrate, 11 mg Cholesterol, 388 mg Sodium, 3.1 g Protein, 2.6 g Fiber.

CUCUMBER SALAD

2 large cucumbers, peeled, seeded and chopped
1/3 C. scallions, minced
1/4 C. white vinegar
1/2 t. sugar
Ground black pepper

Combine all ingredients. Chill. 4 servings.

Nutritional Information: 36 Calories, 0.3 g Fat, 8.2 g Carbohydrate, 0 mg Cholesterol, 6 mg Sodium, 1.7 g Protein, 2 g Fiber, 6.1 g Sugar.

EGGPLANT SALAD

2 eggplants
2 cloves garlic, crushed
1 onion, sliced

1 T. parsley, chopped
1/4 C. low-fat plain yogurt
Salt and pepper, to taste

Pierce eggplants with a fork and grill for 20 minutes, turning frequently. Cool, then peel and chop. Mix with the rest of the ingredients. Serves 4.

Nutritional Information: 95 Calories, 0.8 g Fat, 21 g Carbohydrate, 1 mg Cholesterol, 21 mg Sodium, 4.1 g Protein, 7.5 g Fiber, 12.3 g Sugar.

GREEK SALAD

1 T. red wine vinegar
1 T. fresh lemon juice
2 t. chopped fresh oregano
1/2 t. salt
1/4 t. ground black pepper
2 1/2 T. extra-virgin olive oil
1 large eggplant, peeled and cut
  into 1/2-inch cubes

1 lb. spinach, steamed and torn
  into bite-sized pieces
1 cucumber, peeled, seeded and
  diced
1 tomato, seeded and diced
1/2 red onion, diced
2 T. pitted chopped black Greek
  olives
2 T. crumbled Feta cheese

Preheat oven to 450 degrees F. Lightly coat a baking sheet with olive oil cooking spray. Whisk together the first 5 ingredients. Slowly add the olive oil, while whisking. Set aside. Spread the eggplant cubes on the baking sheet. Spray the eggplant with the olive oil cooking spray. Cook for 10 minutes. Turn and cook 10 more minutes. Set aside and let cool completely. In a salad bowl, add all the ingredients, except the dressing and cheese. Toss. Add the dressing and toss. Sprinkle with the cheese. Serves 8.

Nutritional Information: 88 Calories, 5 g Fat, 9 g Carbohydrate, 2 mg Cholesterol, 245 mg Sodium, 3 g Protein, 3 g Fiber.

TOMATO ASPARAGUS SALAD

1 lb. fresh asparagus, trimmed
4 C. romaine lettuce, torn
4 romaine lettuce leaves

1/3 C. low-fat Italian salad
 dressing
2 T. Parmesan cheese, shredded

Cook asparagus in boiling water for 5 to 6 minutes. Plunge in ice water to cool. Line an 11x7-inch dish with romaine leaves. Top with torn romaine. Arrange asparagus and tomatoes on top and drizzle with the dressing. Sprinkle with the cheese. Chill 1 hour before serving. Serves 6.

Nutritional Information: 100 Calories, 3 g Fat, 16 g Carbohydrate, 459 mg Sodium, 5 g Protein, 5 g Fiber.

SPINACH AND RED POTATOES SALAD

1-10 oz. pkg. fresh spinach, torn
3 small red potatoes, cooked and
 diced
2 hard-boiled eggs, peeled and
 chopped
1/2 C. sliced fresh mushrooms
2 bacon strips, cooked and diced

Save the drippings from the bacon
1/4 C. red onion, chopped
1/2 t. cornstarch
1/4 C. apple juice
2 T. cider vinegar
2 t. sweetener
1/8 t. pepper

Add the first 4 ingredients. In the drippings sauté the onion until tender. Add the rest of the ingredients and bring to a boil for 1 to 2 minutes. Pour over the spinach mixture. Add the bacon and toss. Serves 8.

Nutritional Information: 93 Calories, 5.6 g Fat, 7.2 g Carbohydrate, 58 mg Cholesterol, 99 mg Sodium, 4.6 g Protein, 2.9 g Fiber.

CREAMY POTATO SALAD

4 medium potatoes, cooked tender
  and diced
1 C. sliced celery
1/4 C. finely-chopped onion
2 T. dill pickle relish
1/2 C. light mayonnaise

1/2 C. light sour cream
2 T. skim milk
2 t. prepared mustard
1/2 t. salt
1/4 t. celery seed
1 hard-boiled egg, chopped

Place potatoes, celery, onion and pickle relish in a large bowl. In a small mixing bowl, add the next 6 ingredients. Pour over the potato mixture and toss. Fold in the egg. Cover and refrigerate for at least 4 hours up to 24 hours. Serves 6.

Nutritional Information: 155 Calories, 7 g Fat, 20 g Carbohydrate, 29 mg Cholesterol, 357 mg Sodium, 4 g Protein, 1 g Fiber.

CHICKEN SALAD

4 C. cubed, cooked chicken
1 C. mayonnaise
1 t. paprika
1 1/2 C. dried cranberries
1 C. celery, chopped

2 green onions, chopped
1/2 C. minced green bell pepper
1 C. chopped pecans
1 t. seasoning salt
Pepper, to taste

Add all the ingredients and mix well. Chill 1 hour. Serves 12.

Nutritional Information: 322 Calories, 13.6 g Carbohydrate, 46 mg Cholesterol, 214 mg Sodium, 14 g Protein, 2.5 g Fiber.

SOUTHWEST CHICKEN SALAD

1-15 oz. can black beans, drained
  and rinsed
Salt and pepper, to taste
1/2 C. head cabbage, chopped
1-10 oz. pkg. romaine lettuce, torn
1/2 green bell pepper, chopped
1-8.75 oz. can corn, drained

1/4 C. shredded Cheddar cheese
2 C. skinless, boneless chicken
  breast halves, cut into strips
1 C. finely-crushed blue tortilla
  chips
1/2 C. ranch salad dressing

In a small saucepan over medium heat, cook the beans until heated through. Season with salt and pepper. In a large bowl, add the next 5 ingredients and toss. Top with the beans, chicken, tortilla chips and dressing. Serves 4.

Nutritional Information: 505 Calories, 24.5 g Fat, 46 g Carbohydrate, 58 mg Cholesterol, 1071 mg Sodium, 29.6 g Protein, 13.9 g Fiber.

PINEAPPLE CHICKEN SALAD

4 boneless, skinless chicken
  breasts
1 T. olive oil
1-8 oz. can unsweetened pineapple
  chunks, drained, saving 2 T. juice
2 C. broccoli florets

4 C. fresh baby spinach leaves
1/2 C. thinly-sliced red onions
1/4 C. olive oil
2 T. balsamic vinegar
2 t. sugar
1/4 t. ground cinnamon

Cut each chicken breast into cubes. In a non-stick frying pan, heat the olive oil over medium heat. Add the chicken and cook until golden brown, about 10 minutes. In a large bowl, combine the cooked chicken, pineapple, broccoli, spinach and onions. In a small bowl, whisk the olive oil, vinegar, sugar and cinnamon. Pour over the salad and toss. Serves 8.

Nutritional Information: 187 Calories, 9 g Fat, 8 g Carbohydrate, 41 mg Cholesterol, 75 mg Sodium, 17 g Protein, 2 g Fiber.

CHICKEN AND TOMATO SALAD

1 1/2 T. lemon juice
2 cloves garlic, minced
1/2 t. thyme
1/4 t. salt
1/4 t. pepper
1/8 t. cayenne pepper

1/2 C. nonfat plain yogurt
3 C. cubed, cooked chicken breasts
1 C. thinly-sliced green onion
1/2 C. diced green bell pepper
1/2 C. diced celery
2 C. diced fresh tomatoes

Mix the first 6 ingredients. Beat in the yogurt. Gently fold the chicken and next 3 ingredients in the dressing. Chill. Just before serving, fold in the tomatoes. Serves 6.

Nutritional Information: 192 Calories, 7 g Fat, 13 g Carbohydrate, 549 mg Sodium, 21 g Protein, 2 g Fiber.

GRILLED CHICKEN CAESAR SALAD

2 boneless, skinless chicken
  breasts
3 T. fat-free Italian dressing
6 C. romaine lettuce

1/3 C. Parmesan cheese
1/2 C. plain croutons
1/4 C. fat-free Caesar salad
  dressing

In a bowl, add the chicken and Italian dressing. Cover and place in the refrigerator for 30 minutes, turning the chicken over after 15 minutes. Cook the chicken on the grill. Let rest for 5 minutes before slicing into strips. Mix all the other ingredients and toss with the Caesar dressing. Top the salad with the chicken. Serves 2.

Nutritional Information: 250 Calories, 7 g Fat, 14 g Carbohydrate, 70 mg Cholesterol, 969 mg Sodium, 30 g Protein, 4 g Fiber.

CHICKEN WALDORF SALAD

1/4 C. nonfat plain yogurt
1/4 C. low-fat mayonnaise
1/2 t. honey
Salt and pepper, to taste
1 C. chopped apple, tossed with
  2 t. fresh lemon juice
1/2 C. red grapes, halved
1/2 C. green grapes, halved

1/2 C. celery
2 T. chopped scallion
1 skinless, boneless chicken
  breast, cooked and cubed
1 small cantaloupe, seeds removed
  and cut into 4 wedges
2 T. chopped walnuts

In a large bowl, whisk the first 4 ingredients. Add the rest of the ingredients, except the cantaloupe and walnuts. Place 1/4 of the chicken mixture on the cantaloupe wedges and sprinkle with the walnuts. Serves 4.

Nutritional Information: 251 Calories, 8 g Fat, 164 mg Sodium.

STEAK AND MUSHROOM SALAD

1/2 C. red wine
1 lb. flank steak
12 oz. cremini mushrooms,
  cleaned

6 oz. Gorgonzola cheese, crumbled
Spinach leaves

Place 3 tablespoons of red wine in a large food storage bag. Add the steak. Seal and toss to coat steak. Place the remaining red wine in a large salad bowl. Thinly slice the mushrooms and add to the bowl. Toss to coat. Scatter spinach leaves on top of the mushrooms. Do not toss. Cook the steak on the grill. Let stand 10 minutes and then thinly slice the steak across the grain on a slight diagonal. Toss the mushrooms and spinach in the bowl. Top with steak. Garnish with the cheese. Servings size 4.

Nutritional Information: 398 Calories, 24 g Fat, 12 g Carbohydrate, 34 g Protein.

CRAB SALAD

10 oz. low-fat plain yogurt
1/4 C. reduced-fat mayonnaise
1/3 C. chopped fresh dill
1 t. dried tarragon
2 t. Dijon mustard

1/4 t. salt
1 lb. lump or imitation crabmeat, chopped
2 cucumbers, seeded and chopped
4 scallions, chopped

Mix the first 6 ingredients. Stir in the rest of the ingredients. Cover and refrigerate at least 3 hours. Serves 4.

Nutritional Information: 210 Calories, 6 g Fat, 11 g Carbohydrate, 102 mg Cholesterol, 544 mg Sodium, 24 g Protein, 0 g Fiber.

LOBSTER AND SHRIMP SALAD

4 ears corn, shucked
2 C. finely-diced zucchini
1 C. finely-diced tomato
6 oz. lobster
1/2 lb. shrimp, cooked and peeled
2 T. fresh lemon juice

1/2 t. salt
1/2 t. ground black pepper
2 T. olive oil
1/2 C. slivered fresh basil leaves, divided

Cook the corn in boiling water for 7 minutes. Remove and let cool. Cut the kernels from the cobs and place kernels in a large bowl. Bring water to a boil again and add the zucchini and cook for 2 minutes. Drain and add the zucchini to the bowl with the corn. Toss in the diced tomatoes. Whisk the lemon juice, salt, pepper and oil. Set aside. Cut shrimp in half and chop the lobster. Place seafood in a mixing bowl and add half of the basil. Add 2 tablespoons of the dressing mix to the seafood and toss well. Add remaining basil to the corn mixture and toss. Mix the seafood with the corn mixture. Serves 4.

Nutritional Information: 261 Calories, 10 g Fat, 23 g Carbohydrate, 512 mg Sodium, 24 g Protein, 4 g Fiber.

TUNA PASTA SALAD

2 C. uncooked bow-tie pasta,
cooked as pkg. directions
2-6 oz. cans unsalted white tuna
packed in water, drained
1/4 C. finely-chopped onions

2/3 C. frozen peas, thawed
2/3 C. reduced-fat salad dressing
1/8 t. ground black pepper
4 C. fresh spinach

Drain the pasta and rinse under cold water. Mix all the ingredients, except the spinach, and chill for 2 hours. When ready to serve, add the spinach in a salad bowl and place the pasta mixture on top. Serves 4.

Nutritional Information: 337 Calories, 15 g Fat, 28 g Carbohydrate, 44 mg Cholesterol, 694 mg Sodium, 22 gm Protein, 5 g Fiber.

TUNA SALAD

2-6 oz. cans solid white tuna,
drained well
2 T. minced red bell pepper
3 T. minced red onion
1 clove garlic, minced
1 t. caper, drained and minced
1 T. minced fresh cilantro leaves

1 t. extra-virgin olive oil
Juice of 1 lime
1 C. reduced-fat mayonnaise
1 t. balsamic vinegar
1/4 t. Tabasco sauce
1/2 C. diced tomatoes
Salt and pepper, to taste

Mix the first 6 ingredients. In a small bowl, blend in the next 7 ingredients. Pour over the tuna mixture. Refrigerate for at least 1 hour. Serves 6.

Nutritional Information: 60 Calories, 1 g Fat, 3.9 g Carbohydrate.

GREEK PASTA SALAD

1-16 oz. pkg. penne pasta, cook as
  to pkg. directions
1/4 C. vegetable oil
1 t. lemon juice
1 t. dried basil
1 t. fresh ground pepper

1 t. garlic salt
2 tomatoes, chopped
1 green bell pepper, chopped
1 sweet onion, chopped
1 cucumber, coarsely chopped
1 C. black olives, chopped

Drain pasta and rinse under cold water. In a small bowl, add the next 5 ingredients and mix. Set aside. Mix the rest of the ingredients together. Add the pasta and toss with the dressing. Chill in refrigerator for 30 minutes. Serves 8.

Nutritional Information: 304 Calories, 10.3 g Fat, 46.8 g Carbohydrate, 0 mg Cholesterol, 389 mg Sodium, 8.4 g Protein, 3.7 g Fiber.

CARIBBEAN FRUIT SALAD

1 mango, diced
1 banana, sliced
1/2 C. cubed fresh pineapple
2 T. frozen orange juice
  concentrate, thawed

1 T. rum
1 t. sugar
1 t. imitation coconut flavoring

Mix all ingredients. Let stand at room temperature for 10 minutes. Cover and refrigerate up to 30 minutes. 4 servings.

Nutritional Information: 88 Calories, 0.5 g Fat, 22 g Carbohydrate, 2 mg Sodium, 1 g Protein, 2 g Fiber.

SPICED GRAPE AND YOGURT SALAD

1/4 C. vanilla low-fat yogurt
1/8 t. ground cinnamon
1/8 t. ground cardamom

1 C. seedless green grapes
1 C. seedless red or black grapes

Combine the first 3 ingredients in a bowl and mix. Add the grapes and stir gently. Cover and refrigerate until chilled. Serves 4.

Nutritional Information: 70 Calories, 0.7 g Fat, 16.5 g Carbohydrate, 1 mg Cholesterol, 12 mg Sodium, 1.4 g Protein, 0.9 g Fiber, 15.6 g Sugar.

GRAPEFRUIT AND ORANGE SALAD

2 oranges, peeled, sectioned and
  seeded
1 red grapefruit, peeled, sectioned
  and seeded
1 T. orange juice

2 T. olive oil
1 T. balsamic vinegar
Sweetener, as desired
4 C. greens
2 T. pine nuts

Whisk together the orange juice, olive oil and vinegar. Add sweetener. Pour over the fruit and toss. Sprinkle with the nuts. Serves 4.

Nutritional Information: 166 Calories, 10 g Fat, 19 g Carbohydrate, 0 mg Cholesterol, 7 mg Sodium, 2 g Protein, 4 g Fiber.

PEAR AND SPINACH SALAD

1-16 oz. bag fresh spinach leaves
2 T. crumbled blue cheese
1/4 red onion, thinly sliced
1-16 oz. can pear slices, drained

3 T. balsamic vinegar
1 T. olive oil
Salt and pepper, to taste

Place the spinach leaves in a large bowl and sprinkle with the blue cheese and onion slices. Add the pear slices. In a small saucepan, heat the vinegar and oil to steaming. Immediately pour the dressing over the salad and toss. Season with the salt and pepper. Serves 6.

Nutritional Information: 70 Calories, 3 g Fat, 10 g Carbohydrate, 94 mg Sodium, 3 g Protein, 3 g Fiber.

MAIN
MEALS

NOTES

CHICKEN BREAST WITH SALSA

2 skinless and boneless chicken
  breast halves
Juice of 1 lemon

1/4 C. extra-virgin olive oil
2 t. minced garlic
Salt and pepper, to taste

Place the chicken in a bowl with rest of the ingredients. Cover and refrigerate for 15 minutes, turning once. Remove the chicken from the marinade and grill for 3 to 4 minutes on each side.

Salsa:
1 avocado, diced
1 T. lime juice

1 tomato, diced
2 T. cilantro, chopped

Mix well and serve on top of the chicken. Serves 2.

Nutritional Information: 390 Calories, 25 g Fat, 14 g Carbohydrate, 75 mg Cholesterol, 30 g Protein.

Sexy women have messy kitchens.

CHICKEN PENNE

1 1/2 C. uncooked penne pasta
1 C. chopped asparagus
6 oz. boneless, skinless chicken
  breasts
2 cloves garlic, minced

1-14.5 oz. can diced tomatoes with
  herbs, undrained
1 oz. soft goat cheese, crumbled
1 T. Parmesan cheese

Cook pasta according to directions. Drain and set aside. Steam the asparagus until tender-crisp, about 2 to 3 minutes. Spray a large frying pan with Pam. Add the chicken and garlic and sauté over medium-high heat, about 5 to 7 minutes. Add the tomatoes and simmer 1 minute more. Toss the pasta, chicken, asparagus and goat cheese. Sprinkle with the Parmesan cheese. Serves 2.

Nutritional Information: 455 Calories, 8 g Total Fat, 55 g Carbohydrate, 81 mg Cholesterol, 240 mg Sodium, 41 g Protein, 6.5 g Fiber.

No Bitchin' in the Kitchen.

BLUE CHEESE CHICKEN AND PASTA

8 C. cooked pasta of your choice
1 t. paprika
1/2 t. garlic powder
Salt and pepper, to taste
1 1/2 lbs. boneless, skinless
  chicken breasts, cut into bite-
  sized pieces
1 t. hot sauce

1 C. sliced celery
1 small red onion, chopped
1/2 C. low-fat mayonnaise
1/2 C. low-fat blue cheese salad
  dressing
1 C. skim milk
2 T. blue cheese, crumbled

Sprinkle the chicken with the paprika, garlic powder, salt and pepper. Spray a large non-stick skillet with non-stick cooking spray and heat over medium heat until hot. Add the chicken and sauté until done. Add the hot sauce and stir to coat. Remove the chicken from the skillet. Respray the skillet and heat over medium heat until hot. Add the celery and onion and sauté for 2 minutes. In a bowl, add the mayonnaise, blue cheese dressing and milk. Mix well. Add the chicken, celery, onion, pasta and sauce. Toss to coat and heat through, stirring constantly. Sprinkle with the crumbled blue cheese. Serves 8.

Nutritional Information: 397 Calories, 9 g Fat, 48 g Carbohydrate, 60 mg Cholesterol, 432 mg Sodium, 28 g Protein, 3 g Fiber.

If all else fails.....Cocktails!

CHICKEN CACCIATORE

4 small skinless, boneless chicken breast halves
1-14 1/2 oz. can stewed tomatoes
1 medium green bell pepper, cut into thin strips

1/2 C. sliced fresh mushrooms
1/4 C. chopped onion
1/4 C. red wine
2 t. dried Italian seasonings
1/8 t. black pepper

Spray an unheated large skillet with Pam. Preheat over medium heat. Add the chicken and cook about 6 minutes or until lightly browned. Stir in the rest of the ingredients. Bring to a boil and reduce the heat. Simmer, covered, about 15 minutes. Remove chicken from the skillet and keep the chicken warm. Simmer the tomato mixture, uncovered, about 5 minutes. Place chicken on a serving plate and pour the tomato mixture over. Serves 4.

Nutritional Information: 134 Calories, 3 g Fat, 10 g Carbohydrate, 45 mg Cholesterol, 309 mg Sodium, 18 g Protein, 3 g Fiber.

I gave up jogging.....the ice kept falling out of my glass.

SOUTHWESTERN CHICKEN AND PASTA

1 C. uncooked rigatoni
2 boneless, skinless chicken
  breasts, cut into cubes
1/4 C. salsa
1 1/2 C. canned unsalted tomato
  sauce
1/8 t. garlic powder

1 t. cumin
1/2 t. chili powder
1/2 C. canned black beans, rinsed
  and drained
1/2 C. canned corn
1/4 C. shredded Colby Jack cheese

Cook the rigatoni according to package. Drain. Spray a large skillet with Pam. Over medium heat, sauté the chicken until browned and opaque throughout, 7 to 10 minutes. Stir in the rest of the ingredients, except the cheese. Heat. Add the pasta and gently toss to mix. Sprinkle the cheese over the pasta. Serves 2.

Nutritional Information: 482 Calories, 8 g Total Fat, 3 g Saturated Fat, 59 g Carbohydrate, 81 mg Cholesterol, 700 mg Sodium, 41 g Protein, 8 g Fiber.

I'm only as strong as the cocktails I drink,
the hairspray I use and the friends I have.

CHICKEN AND PENNE WITH BASIL SAUCE

1 1/4 C. reduced-sodium chicken broth
4 t. cornstarch
1/8 t. black pepper
2 C. pkg. dried penne pasta
1 medium red bell pepper, cut into thin strips
1 medium yellow bell pepper, cut into thin strips
3 cloves garlic, minced
1 T. cooking oil
12 oz. skinless, boneless chicken breast halves, cut into 1-inch cubes
1/4 C. lightly-packed fresh basil leaves, cut into thin shreds
2 T. finely-shredded Parmesan cheese

Stir together the chicken broth, cornstarch and black pepper. Set aside. Cook pasta according to package directions, omitting any oil and salt. Drain. Cover and keep warm. Spray a large skillet with Pam. Preheat over medium heat. Add the peppers and garlic. Stir-fry for 3 minutes, or until crisp-tender. Remove from the skillet. Add the oil to the skillet. Increase the heat to medium-high. Add the chicken and stir-fry for 3 to 4 minutes. Stir in the chicken broth mixture. Cook and stir until thickened and bubbly. Return the peppers to the skillet. Add the basil. Cook and stir for 2 more minutes. Toss with the pasta and sprinkle with the Parmesan cheese. Serves 4.

Nutritional Information: 330 Calories, 8 g Fat, 39 g Carbohydrate, 47 mg Cholesterol, 282 mg Sodium, 24 g Protein, 1 g Fiber.

Life is too short to drink cheap wine.

FRIED CHICKEN

1 C. plain bread crumbs
1 t. dill
1 t. Italian blend spice

1/2 C. skim milk
4-4 oz. boneless, skinless chicken
  breasts

Preheat oven to 350 degrees F. Place the bread crumbs with the dill and Italian spice and milk in separate bowls. Drag the chicken through the milk, then bread crumbs turning until each is coated completely. Place on a foil-covered baking sheet and bake for 25 minutes. Serves 4.

Nutritional Information: 230 Calories, 4 g Fat, 1 g Saturated Fat, 19 g Carbohydrate, 65 mg Cholesterol, 280 mg Sodium, 27 gm Protein, 1 g Fiber, 1 g Sugar.

MAPLE BARBEQUED CHICKEN

3 T. pure maple syrup
3 T. bottled chili sauce
1 T. cider vinegar
2 t. Dijon mustard

4 boneless chicken breast halves
Olive oil
Salt and pepper, to taste

Stir the first 4 ingredients together. Brush the chicken with oil, salt, pepper and the sauce. Cook on the grill, brushing generously with the remaining sauce, for 10 minutes or until done. Serves 4.

Nutritional Information: 142 Calories, 4.5 g Fat, 10 g Carbohydrate, 93 mg Sodium, 20 g Protein, 0 g Fiber, 3 Weight Watcher Points.

FAJITAS

2 green bell peppers, sliced
1 red bell pepper, sliced
1 onion, thinly sliced
1 C. fresh mushrooms, sliced
2 C. chicken meat, cooked and
  diced

1-0.7 oz. pkg. dry Italian-style
  salad dressing mix
10-12-inch flour tortillas
Shredded Cheddar cheese
Diced tomatoes
Shredded lettuce

Sauté peppers and onion in a small amount of oil until tender. Add the mushrooms and chicken. Continue to cook on low heat until heated through. Stir in the dry salad dressing mix and blend thoroughly. Warm the tortillas and roll the chicken mixture inside. Add the rest of the ingredients on top. Serves 10.

Nutritional Information: 443 Calories, 9.6 g Fat, 69.4 g Carbohydrate, 21 mg Cholesterol, 828 mg Sodium, 18.4 g Protein, 4.8 g Fiber.

SLOW-COOKER LEMON CHICKEN

4 boneless, skinless chicken breast
  halves
2 T. lemon-pepper seasoning
1-16 oz. bag fresh soup vegetables,
  chopped

1-10 3/4 oz. can reduced-fat cream
  of chicken soup
1 t. dried rosemary, crushed

Coat chicken with the lemon-pepper seasoning. Spray a skillet with Pam. Place over a medium-high stove. Add the chicken and cook 5 minutes, turning once. Place the chicken in the slow-cooker. Add the vegetables. In a bowl, combine soup, half a soup can of water and the rosemary. Pour over the chicken. Cover and cook on low 8 hours or 4 hours on high. Serves 4.

Nutritional Information: 205 Calories, 4 g Fat, 18 g Carbohydrate, 55 mg Cholesterol, 940 mg Sodium, 21 g Protein, 3 g Fiber.

CRANBERRY CHICKEN

Stacy Saba, Chandler, AZ

4 chicken breast halves, boneless
  and skinless
1/4 C. soy sauce
3 T. brown sugar
1/2 t. ground ginger
1/4 C. cranberry vinegar

1 t. freshly-squeezed lemon juice
1/2 green bell pepper, cored,
  seeded and chopped
2 cloves garlic, chopped
Cooked rice

Preheat oven to 350 degrees F. when ready to bake. Place chicken in a shallow pan. In a medium bowl, combine the rest of the ingredients, except the rice. Pour over the chicken and cover. Marinate in the refrigerator 1 hour or overnight. Place in a glass baking dish and bake for 30 minutes. Serve with the rice. Serves 4.

Nutritional Information: 186 Calories, 3 g Fat, 11 g Carbohydrate.

BLUE CHEESE CHICKEN

1 t. dried basil
1/4 t. pepper
1/8 t. salt

4 boneless, skinless chicken
  breasts
1 oz. crumbled blue cheese
1 green onion, finely chopped

Sprinkle the first 3 ingredients over the chicken. Heat a skillet with a vegetable oil spray. Cook the chicken for 6 minutes on each side. Remove the skillet from the heat. Sprinkle the chicken with the blue cheese and green onion. Let stand until the cheese has melted slightly. Serves 4.

Nutritional Information: 154 Calories, 3.5 g Fat, 1 g Carbohydrate, 71 mg Cholesterol, 247 mg Sodium, 28 g Protein.

CITRUS CHICKEN

3 T. fresh orange juice
2 T. canned unsweetened
  pineapple juice
2 T. fresh lime juice
2 T. chopped fresh oregano
1 T. olive oil
1 t. ground cumin

1 t. chili powder
1 garlic clove, chopped
6 dashes hot sauce
Salt and pepper, to taste
6 bone-in chicken thigh, skin and
  fat removed

Preheat oven to 375 degrees F. Add all the ingredients, expect the chicken, in a blender. Purée until smooth. Arrange the chicken in a baking dish and brush with half the citrus mixture. Bake the chicken for 30 to 35 minutes, occasionally brushing the chicken with the citrus mixture. Serves 6.

Nutritional Information: 385 Calories, 15 g Fat, 86 mg Sodium.

OVEN-FRIED CHICKEN

1 C. whole wheat bread crumbs
1/4 C. grated Parmesan cheese
1/4 C. finely-chopped almonds
2 T. chopped parsley
1 clove garlic, crushed
1 t. salt

1/4 t. dried thyme
Pinch of black pepper
1/4 C. extra-virgin olive oil
2 lbs. boneless, skinless chicken
  breasts, pounded to 1/2-inch
  thickness and cut into 12 pieces

Preheat the oven to 400 degrees F. Add the first 8 ingredients in a bowl and mix thoroughly. Place the oil in a shallow dish. Dip the chicken first in the oil and then dredge in the crumb mixture. Place the chicken in a shallow baking pan. Bake for 25 minutes. Serves 6.

Nutritional Information: 383 Calories, 16 g Fat, 15 g Carbohydrate, 91 mg Cholesterol, 730 mg Sodium, 41 g Protein, 1 g Fiber.

DEVILED CHICKEN BREAST

2 T. Italian-seasoned bread crumbs
4-4 oz. skinned, boned chicken
  breast halves
1 T. olive oil
1/2 c. dry white wine
1/4 t. salt

1/4 t. black pepper
1-4 oz. jar whole mushrooms,
  drained
1 T. lemon juice
1 T. honey mustard

Place the crumbs in a heavy-duty, zip-top plastic bag. Add the chicken and shake until well coated. Heat the oil in a skillet over medium heat. Add the chicken and cook for 3 minutes on each side. Add the wine and next 4 ingredients and cover. Reduce the heat and simmer 15 minutes. Remove the chicken and mushrooms with a slotted spoon and place on a serving platter. Add the lemon juice and mustard to the skillet. Stir. Cook 1 minute. Serve with the chicken. Serves 4.

Nutritional Information: 215 Calories, 5 g Fat, 8.4 g Carbohydrate, 66 mg Cholesterol, 548 mg Sodium, 27.8 g Protein, 0.3 g Fiber.

PSYCHO CHICKEN

3 1/2 lbs. whole chicken
1 T. cider vinegar
1 1/2 t. dried thyme
1/4 t. salt

1/4 t. black pepper
3 garlic cloves, minced
1/2 C. dry white wine

Preheat oven to 325 degrees F. Combine the vinegar, thyme, salt, pepper and garlic. Brush all over the chicken. Place breast-side up on a broiler pan. Pour the wine over the chicken. Bake for 1 hour and 45 minutes. Let stand 10 minutes. Discard the skin. Serves 5.

Nutritional Information: 139 Calories, 3.1 g Fat, 1.3 g Carbohydrate, 204 mg Sodium, 23.2 g Protein, 0.3 g Fiber.

TURKEY LOAF

2 t. vegetable oil
1 C. finely-chopped onion
3/4 C. finely-chopped carrot
1/2 C. finely-chopped green
  onions
1/2 C. finely-chopped celery
1/2 C. finely-chopped red bell
  pepper
2 garlic cloves, minced
2 1/2 lbs. ground turkey breast
1 C. dry bread crumbs

1/3 C. ketchup
1 t. salt
1 t. pepper
1/4 t. nutmeg
1/4 t. cumin
1/4 t. coriander
4 egg whites, lightly beaten
Vegetable cooking spray
1/2 C. ketchup
3 T. brown sugar

Preheat oven to 350 degrees F. Heat the oil in a skillet over medium heat until hot. Add the onion and next 5 ingredients. Sauté 5 minutes until tender. Combine the onion mixture to the ground turkey and next 8 ingredients in a large bowl. Stir until mixed. Shape meat in a 9x5-inch loaf pan. Bake for 30 minutes. Let stand 10 minutes before slicing. Serves 12.

Nutritional Information: 186 Calories, 2 g Fat, 16.7 g Carbohydrate, 59 mg Cholesterol, 533 mg Sodium, 24.4 g Protein, 1.5 g Fiber.

What time is it? Wine-thirty!

MUSTARD-MAPLE PORK TENDERLOIN

3 T. Dijon mustard, divided
1/2 t. kosher salt
1/2 t. freshly-ground pepper
1 lb. pork tenderloin, trimmed

2 t. canola oil
1/4 C. cider vinegar
2 T. maple syrup
1 1/2 t. chopped sage

Preheat oven to 425 degrees F. Combine 1 tablespoon mustard, salt and pepper in a small bowl. Rub all over the pork. Heat the oil in a large ovenproof skillet over medium-high heat. Add the pork and brown on all sides, 3 to 5 minutes. Transfer the pan to the oven and roast for about 15 minutes. Transfer to a cutting board and let rest for 5 minutes. Place the skillet over medium-high heat. Add the vinegar and boil for about 30 seconds. Whisk in the maple syrup and 2 tablespoons mustard. Bring to a boil, reduce heat to simmer and cook until the sauce is thickened, about 5 minutes. Slice the pork and top with the sauce. Serves 4.

Nutritional Information: 225 Calories, 7 g Fat, 9 g Carbohydrate, 78 mg Cholesterol, 479 mg Sodium, 28 g Protein, 0 g Fiber, 489 mg Potassium.

Prozac, schmozac, haven't these people heard of a good martini.

PORK MEDALLIONS WITH RED PEPPERS

2 t. olive oil
8-2 oz. boneless center-cut loin
  pork chops
1/4 t. dried Italian seasoning
1/8 t. salt
1/8 t. pepper
2 C. red bell pepper strips

1 C. fat-free, less-sodium chicken
  broth
2 T. tomato paste
1/4 t. dried thyme
1/4 t. dried rubbed sage
1-14 oz. can artichoke hearts,
  drained

Spray a non-stick skillet with cooking spray. Add the oil and heat over medium-high heat. Sprinkle the pork with the Italian seasoning, salt and pepper. Add the pork to the skillet. Cook 1 minute on each side. Remove from the skillet. Add the red bell pepper strips to the skillet. Sauté for 2 minutes. In a small bowl, combine the broth, tomato paste, thyme and sage. Whisk. Return the pork to the skillet and add the broth mixture and artichoke hearts. Cover, reduce heat and simmer for 8 minutes. Remove the pork and keep warm. Increase the heat to medium-high. Cook the artichoke mixture for 2 minutes. Spoon over the pork. Serves 4.

Nutritional Information: 239 Calories, 8 g Total Fat, 3 g Saturated Fat, 16 g Carbohydrate, 814 mg Sodium, 27 g Protein, 5 g Fiber, 5 Weight Watcher Points.

You say "potato." I say "vodka."

CHILI VERDE BURRITOS

1 lb. pork tenderloin, cut into
  1-inch pieces
1 lb. fresh tomatillos, drained
2 carrots, coarsely chopped
1 potato, peeled and cut into
  1-inch pieces
4 cloves garlic, minced
2-7 oz. jars green chili salsa
1-7 oz. can diced green chili,
  drained

1/2 t. salt
1/4 t. red pepper
12-8 oz. whole wheat tortillas,
  warmed
2 medium tomatoes, chopped
1 C. snipped fresh chives
1/2 C. snipped and loosely-packed
  fresh cilantro

Spray a Dutch oven with Pam. Heat over medium-high heat. Add the pork. Cook and stir until the pork is no longer pink. Add the next 4 ingredients and cook and stir about 7 minutes more. Add the salsa, chili peppers, salt and pepper. Bring to a boil, then reduce the heat. Cover and simmer for 30 minutes. Let your guest assemble their own burritos. Makes 12 burritos, 2 per serving.

Nutritional Information: 380 Calories, 10 g Fat, 21% Calories from Fat, 49 mg Cholesterol.

At my age, happy hour is a nap.

PORK CHOPS SUPREME

4 pork chops, about 3/4-inch thick
Salt and pepper
4 thin onion slices

4 thin lemon slices
1/4 C. packed brown sugar
1/4 C. ketchup

Preheat oven to 350 degrees F. Sprinkle both sides of the chops with the salt and pepper. Place chops in an ungreased shallow baking pan. Top each pork chop with an onion slice, a lemon slice, 1 tablespoon brown sugar and 1 tablespoon ketchup. Cover and cook for 20 minutes. Mix the rest of brown sugar and ketchup. Uncover and cook, spooning sauce over the chops occasionally, for 30 minutes. Serves 4.

Nutritional Information: 157 Calories, 3 g Fat.

Better to have loved and lost than to have
spent your entire life with a psycho.

STUFFED PORK

Filling:

2 T. chopped parsley
1 1/2 T. chopped fresh sage
1 T. chopped fresh rosemary
3 cloves garlic, minced

3 T. extra-virgin olive oil
2 t. Dijon mustard
1/4 t. salt
1/4 t. ground black pepper

Pork Loin:

2 lbs. center loin pork roast,
    butterfly
3/4 t. salt

1/2 t. black pepper
1 T. extra-virgin olive oil

Preheat oven to 350 degrees F. Mix all the filling ingredients together. Sprinkle the top side of the butterflied loin with half of the salt and pepper. Spread the filling evenly across the loin, leaving a 1/2-inch border along the edge where you made the first cut. Beginning at the opposite edge, roll the loin up to wrap the filling. Using kitchen twine, tie the loin every 1 1/2-inch to hold its shape. Rub the loin with the oil and sprinkle with remaining salt and pepper. Place the loin in a roasting pan. Roast for 1 hour, or until a thermometer inserted in the center registers 155 degrees F. Let stand for 10 minutes before carving. Serves 6.

Nutritional Information: 306 Calories, 19 g Fat, 1 g Carbohydrate, 9 mg Cholesterol, 506 mg Sodium, 31 g Protein, 0 g Fiber.

SESAME PORK TENDERLOIN

2-1 lb. pork tenderloin
1/3 C. extra-virgin olive oil
1/4 C. sesame seeds
1 stalk celery, chopped
2 T. chopped onion
1 C. whole wheat bread crumbs

1 t. lemon juice
1 t. Worcestershire sauce
1/2 t. salt
1/2 t. dried thyme
1/8 t. black pepper

Preheat oven to 325 degrees F. Cut each tenderloin almost through lengthwise, then flatten. Heat the oil in a skillet over medium-high heat. Add the sesame seeds, celery and onion and cook, stirring frequently, for 3 minutes. Add the bread crumbs, lemon juice, Worcestershire sauce, salt, thyme and pepper. Toss lightly. Spread the stuffing on the cut surface of 1 tenderloin. Place the second tenderloin, cut-side down on top of the stuffing. Fasten the tenderloins together with kitchen string. Place in an open pan. Roast for 1 hour and 20 minutes, or until a thermometer inserted in the center registers 155 degrees F. Let stand for 10 minutes before slicing. Serves 6.

Nutritional Information: 377 Calories, 18 g Fat, 15 g Carbohydrate, 114 mg Cholesterol, 442 mg Sodium, 35 g Protein, 0 g Fiber.

A great friend always remembers your birthday but forgets which one.

GARLIC PORK WITH BASIL

3/4 lb. lean pork tenderloin
1 t. vegetable oil
1/4 C. chopped fresh basil

1/4 C. chicken broth
1/8 t. cayenne pepper
3 cloves garlic, crushed

Trim the fat from the pork. Cut pork crosswise into 8 pieces. Flatten each piece of pork to 1/4-inch thickness between waxed paper. Heat the oil in a skillet over medium-high heat. Add the pork and cook for 3 minutes, turning once, until brown. Stir in the remaining ingredients. Heat to boiling, reduce heat, cover and simmer for 5 minutes or until pork is tender. Serves 4.

Nutritional Information: 115 Calories, 3 g Fat, 2 g Carbohydrate, 55 mg Cholesterol, 90 mg Sodium, 18 g Protein.

PORK TENDERLOIN

2 T. Dijon mustard
1 T. chopped fresh rosemary
   leaves
1 T. chopped fresh oregano
2 t. cider vinegar
1/4 t. pepper

1 lb. pork tenderloin, fat trimmed
1 1/4 C. fat-free, low-sodium
   chicken broth
2 T. all-fruit marmalade
1 C. uncooked instant brown rice

Preheat the oven to 350 degrees F. Mix the first 5 ingredients. Brush over the pork. Place pork in a baking dish. Bake for 40 to 45 minutes or until the internal temperature reaches 160 degrees F. Let the pork rest 10 minutes before cutting. In a saucepan, bring the broth and marmalade to a boil. Stir in the rice. Reduce the heat and simmer, covered, for 10 minutes. Serves 4.

Nutritional Information: 252 Calories, 5 g Fat, 24 g Carbohydrate, 63 mg Cholesterol, 211 mg Sodium, 26 g Protein.

WHOLE WHEAT PENNE
WITH BROCCOLI AND SAUSAGE

12 oz. whole wheat pasta
1 large bunch broccoli, cut into
  florets
12 oz. hot Italian turkey, sliced on
  the diagonal

1 pt. grape tomatoes, cut in half
1/2 C. fresh basil leaves, chopped
1/4 C. grated Romano cheese

Heat a large saucepan of salted water to boiling on high. Add the pasta and cook as label directs, adding the broccoli when 3 minutes of cooking time remain. Reserve 1/2 cup cooking water. Drain. Cook sausage on medium 7 to 8 minutes until it begins to brown, stirring occasionally. Add the tomatoes and cook 5 minutes longer, stirring. Stir in the pasta, broccoli and 1/4 cup pasta cooking water into the sausage mixture in a skillet. Heat. Remove from the heat and stir in the basil and cheese. Serves 4.

Nutritional Information: 505 Calories, 13 g Fat, 74 g Carbohydrate, 71 mg Cholesterol, 760 mg Sodium, 32 g Protein, 10 g Fiber.

Are my hot flashes causing global warming?

MEAT LOAF

2 t. canola oil
1 medium sweet onion, chopped
1-12 oz. bottle dark or amber beer
1 t. dried thyme
1 t. dry mustard
3/4 t. salt
1/8 t. ground pepper

1 1/4 lbs. 95% lean ground beef
1 1/4 lbs. 93% lean ground turkey
1 C. fresh whole wheat bread
   crumbs
1/4 C. chopped fresh parsley
1 large egg, lightly beaten
1 egg white, lightly beaten

Preheat oven to 375 degrees F. Coat an 8 1/2x4 1/2-inch loaf pan with cooking spray. Heat the oil in a skillet over medium-high heat. Add the onion and cook, stirring often, until translucent and starting to turn brown, about 5 minutes. Pour in the beer and increase heat to high. Bring to a vigorous boil and cook until the liquid is quite syrupy and reduces to about 3/4 cup, about 8 to 10 minutes. Transfer to a large bowl. Stir in the thyme, dry mustard, salt and pepper. Let cool for 10 minutes. Add the beef, turkey, bread crumbs, parsley, egg and egg whites to the onion mixture. Mix thoroughly and transfer to the pan. Bake for 1 hour and 20 minutes. Lest rest 5 minutes; drain and slice. Serves 8.

Nutritional Information: 259 Calories, 9 g Fat, 2 g Saturated Fat, 2 g Mono Fat, 11 g Carbohydrate, 105 mg Cholesterol, 339 mg Sodium, 31 g Protein, 2 g Fiber, 51 mg Potassium.

A good lawyer knows the law. A great lawyer knows the judge.

JACKIE'S MEAT LOAF

1 C. chopped onion
1 C. chopped green bell pepper
3 T. minced fresh parsley
1 t. pepper
3/4 t. salt
2 garlic cloves, minced

1 egg, lightly beaten
1 slice white bread, torn into small
  pieces
1 1/2 lbs. ground round
1/3 C. ketchup

Preheat oven to 350 degrees F. Add the first 8 ingredients and mix. Crumble the meat into the mixture. Pack mixture into a 9x5-inch loaf pan coated with cooking spray. Spread the ketchup over the meat. Bake for 1 hour. Let meat loaf stand in pan 10 minutes. Cut into 6 pieces. Serving size 1 piece.

Nutritional Information: 220 Calories, 6.9 g Fat, 10.8 g Carbohydrate, 101 mg Cholesterol, 552 mg Sodium, 27.4 g Protein, 1.4 g Fiber.

PIZZA MEAT LOAF

Paula Green, Dallas, TX

1 lb. extra lean ground beef
1/4 C. pizza sauce
1 oz. grated part-skim Mozzarella
  cheese

1/2 C. thin sliced vegetables of
  your liking

Preheat oven to 425 degrees F. Spray a 9-inch pie plate with non-stick cooking spray. Pat the meat into the pie pan. Bake for 12 to 14 minutes. Drain. Top with rest of the ingredients. Return to the oven for 5 minutes. Serves 4.

Nutritional Information: 250 Calories, 15 g Fat.

ZUCCHINI LASAGNA

5 zucchini (1 1/2 lbs.)
1/2 lb. 90% lean ground beef
1-8 oz. can tomato sauce
1/2 t. basil
1/2 t. oregano
1/4 t. salt

1/8 t. garlic powder
1 C. low-fat cottage cheese
2 egg whites
1/4 C. dry bread crumbs
3/4 C. part-skim Mozzarella
  cheese, shredded

Preheat oven to 350 degrees F. Slice unpeeled zucchini lengthwise to make lasagna noodle-like strips. Cook zucchini in water until translucent and tender. Drain. Cook the beef and drain. Return to the skillet. Add the tomato sauce, basil, oregano, salt and garlic powder. Simmer for 5 minutes. Combine the cottage cheese and egg whites in a small bowl. In an 8-inch square baking pan, layer half of each, zucchini to cover the bottom of the pan, bread crumbs, meat mixture, cottage cheese mixture and Mozzarella cheese. Repeat with the rest. Cover with foil. Bake for 30 minutes. Serves 6.

Nutritional Information: 177 Calories, 6 g Fat, 12 g Carbohydrate, 37 mg Cholesterol, 608 mg Sodium, 19 g Protein, 1 g Dietary Fiber.

All you need to start an asylum is an
empty room and the right kind of people.

LAZY LASAGNA

Grace Qualls, Lafayette, LA

1 lb. ground round
1-26 oz. jar low-fat spaghetti sauce
1-16 oz. carton fat-free cottage
  cheese
2 T. grated Parmesan cheese

Cooking spray
1-8 oz. pkg. precooked lasagna
  noodles
1 C. preshredded reduced-fat mild
  Mozzarella cheese

Preheat oven to 350 degrees F. Cook the meat in a non-stick skillet over medium-high heat until browned, stirring to crumble. Drain well and return meat to the pan. Add the sauce and bring to a boil. Reduce heat and simmer 5 minutes. Combine cottage and Parmesan cheeses in a bowl and set aside. Spread 1/2 cup meat mixture in bottom of a 13x9-inch baking dish coated with the cooking spray. Arrange 4 noodles over the meat and top with half of the cottage cheese mixture, 1 cup meat mixture and 1/3 cup Mozzarella cheese. Repeat, ending with noodles. Spread remaining meat mixture over the noodles. Cover and bake for 30 minutes. Uncover and sprinkle with the remaining cheese. Bake 5 more minutes. Let stand 10 minutes before serving. Serves 9.

Nutritional Information: 275 Calories, 6.2 g Fat, 26.1 g Carbohydrate, 43 mg Cholesterol, 584 mg Sodium, 28.1 g Protein, 1.9 g Fiber.

At my age, "getting lucky" means finding my car in the parking lot.

TWENTY-MINUTE LASAGNA

3/4 lb. ground beef, cooked and
 drained
2 pkg. dry spaghetti sauce mix
1 oz. pkg. dry mushroom gravy
 mix
2-6 oz. cans tomato paste

4 C. water
2 T. vegetable oil
1-16 oz. pkg. lasagna noodles,
 cooked according to directions
1-16 oz. pkg. Mozzarella cheese,
 shredded

Preheat oven to 350 degrees F. In a deep skillet, add the sauce mix, gravy mix, tomato paste, water and oil. Bring to a boil and stir in the ground beef. Reduce the heat and simmer 20 minutes. In a baking dish, layer the noodles, sauce and cheese, repeat layers, ending with the cheese. Bake for 20 minutes. Serves 12.

Nutritional Information: 263 Calories, 7.2 g Fat, 38.7 g Carbohydrate, 20 mg Cholesterol, 1000 mg Sodium, 12.4 g Protein, 2.7 g Fiber.

SPAGHETTI MEAT SAUCE

12 oz. 90% lean ground beef
1 C. diced onion
1/2 green bell pepper
1/2 t. minced garlic
1 t. cinnamon
1/4 t. black pepper

1-8 oz. can tomato sauce, unsalted
1-8 oz. can mushroom stems and
 pieces, drained
2 T. Worcestershire sauce
1 t. Italian seasoning

Place in a skillet the ground beef and brown. Drain off all fat. Transfer to a colander and rinse under hot water. Pat dry with a paper towel. Spray the skillet with Pam. Sauté the onion, green pepper and garlic until tender. Return the beef to the skillet with the vegetables and add the rest of the ingredients. Bring to a boil and simmer gently for 15 minutes. Serve over your favorite pasta. Serves 6.

Nutritional Information: 129 Calories, 5 g Fat, 8 g Carbohydrate, 38 mg Cholesterol, 295 mg Sodium, 2 g Dietary Fiber.

HAMBURGER MUSHROOM PIZZA

1-16 oz. loaf unsliced Italian bread
1/2 C. traditional bottled pizza
  sauce
8 slices onions, separated into
  rings
1 C. presliced fresh mushrooms

6 oz. lean ground meat
1 t. dried Italian seasoning
1/2 t. garlic powder
1/4 t. dried crushed red pepper
1 1/2 C. preshredded part-skim
  Mozzarella and Cheddar cheese

Preheat oven to 500 degrees F. Cut the bread in half horizontally. Place both halves of bread, cut-side up, on a large baking sheet. Spread the pizza sauce on both pieces. Place the onion rings and mushrooms evenly over each half. Crumble the beef and sprinkle over the bread. Sprinkle the Italian seasoning, garlic powder and red pepper evenly over the bread. Top with the cheese. Bake for 9 minutes. Slice each half into 3 pieces. Serves 6.

Nutritional Information: 301 Calories, 9.7 g Fat, 35.4 g Carbohydrate, 31 mg Cholesterol, 542 mg Sodium, 15.1 g Protein, 2 g Fiber.

In wine there is truth. In beer there is strength.
In water there is bacteria.

LOADED TWICE-BAKED POTATOES

4 medium russet potatoes
8 oz. 90% lean ground meat
1 C. broccoli florets, finely
  chopped
1 C. water

1 C. reduced-fat Cheddar cheese,
  shredded and divided
1/2 C. reduced-fat sour cream
1/2 t. salt
1/4 t. ground pepper
3 scallions, sliced

Pierce potatoes all over with a fork. Place in the microwave and cook at 50% power, turning once, for 20 minutes or until potatoes are soft. Brown meat in a skillet over medium-high heat, stirring often. Transfer to a large bowl. Increase heat to high, add the broccoli and water to the skillet; cover and cook until tender, 4 to 5 minutes. Drain the broccoli and add to the meat. Carefully cut off the top third of the potatoes. Scoop the insides out into a medium bowl. Place the potato shells in a small baking dish. Add 1/2 cup of the Cheddar cheese, sour cream, salt and pepper to the insides of the potatoes. Mash with a fork. Add the scallion, broccoli and meat to the mashed potatoes. Place 1/4 of the mixture to each shell. Top with the remaining Cheddar cheese. Microwave on high until the filling is hot and the cheese is melted. Serves 4.

Nutritional Information: 366 Calories, 12 g Fat, 6 g Saturated Fat, 4 g Mono Fat, 41 g Carbohydrate, 54 mg Cholesterol, 535 mg Sodium, 24 g Protein, 5 g Fiber, 1280 mg Potassium.

My party affiliation is cocktail!

ONE-DISH SKILLET DINNER

1 t. olive oil
1 bell pepper, thinly sliced
1 onion, thinly sliced
2 C. fat-free, no-salt-added beef
  broth
12 oz. cubed lean beef, cooked

2 t. Worcestershire sauce
1 t. dried oregano
1/4 tsp. pepper
4 oz. dried whole wheat pasta
1 C. broccoli florets

Heat a large skillet over medium heat. Add the oil. Cook the bell pepper and onion for 3 to 4 minutes, stirring occasionally. Stir in the broth, beef, Worcestershire sauce, oregano and pepper. Increase the heat to medium-high and bring to a simmer. Stir in the pasta. Reduce the heat and simmer, covered, for 5 minutes. Stir in the broccoli. Continue cooking for 5 more minutes. Serves 4.

Nutritional Information: 280 Calories, 5 g Fat, 28 g Carbohydrate, 47 mg Cholesterol, 61 mg Sodium, 32 g Protein.

A good friend will bail you out of jail. A true friend will be sitting next to you, saying "Damn, that was fun!"

YANKEE POT ROAST

2 t. olive oil
1-4 lb. boneless chuck roast,
   trimmed
1 T. kosher salt
1 T. cracked black pepper
2 C. chopped onion
2 C. low-salt beef broth

1/4 C. ketchup
2 T. Worcestershire sauce
1 C. chopped plum tomato
1 1/2 lbs. small red potatoes
1 lb. carrots, peeled and cut into
   1-inch pieces
2 T. fresh lemon juice

Preheat oven to 300 degrees F. Heat the oil in a large Dutch oven over medium-high heat. Sprinkle with the salt and pepper. Add the roast, browning on all sides, about 8 minutes. Remove from the pan. Add the onion to the pan and sauté 8 minutes. Return the roast to the pan. Combine the broth, ketchup and Worcestershire sauce and pour over the roast. Add the tomato and bring to a simmer. Cover and bake for 2 1/2 hours. Add the potatoes and carrots; cover and bake 30 more minutes. Stir in the lemon juice. Serves 10.

Nutritional Information: 290 Calories, 8.4 g Fat, 20 g Carbohydrate, 92 mg Cholesterol, 756 mg Sodium, 32.9 g Protein, 3 g Fiber.

Middle age is when your narrow waist and broad mind exchange places.

BAKED PENNE WITH MEAT SAUCE

8 oz. dried penne pasta, cooked
  according to pkg. directions
1-14 oz. can whole Italian-style
  tomatoes
1/2-6 oz. can tomato paste
1/4 C. dry red wine
1/2 t. sugar

1/2 t. dried oregano
1/4 t. black pepper
1 lb. lean ground beef
1/4 C. chopped onion
1/4 C. sliced pitted black olives
1/2 C. shredded reduced-fat
  Mozzarella cheese

Preheat oven to 375 degrees F. Drain the pasta. In a blender, add the undrained tomatoes, tomato paste, wine, sugar, oregano and pepper. Cover and blend until smooth, then set aside. In a large skillet, cook the ground beef until brown. Drain off the fat. Stir in the tomato mixture and bring to a boil. Reduce the heat, cover and simmer for 10 minutes. Stir in pasta and olives. Spoon the mixture into a 2-quart casserole and bake, uncovered, for 30 minutes. Sprinkle with cheese and bake, uncovered, for about 5 more minutes. Serve 6.

Nutritional Information: 339 Calories, 11 g Total Fat, 4 g Saturated Fat, 33 g Carbohydrate, 349 mg Sodium, 24 g Protein, 3 g Fiber, 7 Weight Watcher Points.

*A Southern lady doesn't need a man to
make her happy.....but a maid is essential.*

STIR-FRY

1/2 lb. lean beef, cut into 1/4-inch
  strips
1 small onion, sliced
1 t. chopped garlic
2 C. fresh broccoli flowerets

1 C. sliced carrots
1 C. sliced mushrooms
1 t. soy sauce
4 T. water

Spray a skillet with non-stick coating. Add the meat and garlic and cook. Remove and keep warm. Stir-fry carrots and onions until carrots are partially done. Add the water as needed to prevent sticking. Add the rest of the ingredients and stir-fry until the vegetables are done to your liking. Add the meat. Serve with rice (not included in the calorie count). Serves 4.

Nutritional Information: 150 Calories, 5 g Fat.

HOBO STEW

Geri Baker, Atlanta, GA

1 1/2 lbs. round steak, cut into
  1-inch cubes
1-16 oz. can tomatoes
1-8 oz. can tomato sauce
1 onion, sliced
1 t. Worcestershire sauce
1/2 t. basil

1/4 t. rosemary
1/4 t. pepper
4 medium potatoes, cut into
  1/2-inch cubes
1-10 oz. pkg. frozen mixed
  vegetables

Combine all ingredients in a 3-quart crock-pot. Cook on low setting for 8 to 10 hours. Serves 6.

Nutritional Information: 290 Calories, 7 g Fat, 28 g Carbohydrate, 70 mg Cholesterol, 437 mg Sodium, 29 g Protein, 6 g Dietary Fiber.

VEAL WITH SPINACH AND FETTUCCINE

3/4 lb. thin slices lean veal round
  steak
1 C. sliced fresh mushrooms
1/4 C. chopped shallots
1 C. beef broth

2 t. cornstarch
1/8 t. pepper
1-10 oz. pkg. frozen chopped
  spinach, thawed & well drained
2 C. hot cooked fettuccine

Cut veal crosswise into 1/4-inch strips. Spray a non-stick skillet with non-stick cooking spray. Sauté the veal, mushrooms and shallots over medium-high heat 3 to 5 minutes. Mix the broth, cornstarch and pepper. Stir the broth mixture and spinach into the skillet. Heat to boiling, stirring constantly. Boil and stir 1 minute. Serve over the fettuccine. Serves 4.

Nutritional Information: 255 Calories, 7 g Fat, 23 g Carbohydrate, 55 mg Cholesterol, 190 mg Sodium, 20 g Protein.

SPICY PEPPER SHRIMP

1-3 1/2 oz. bag boil-in-bag long-
  grain rice, cooked according to
  directions
1 T. olive oil
1 C. chopped yellow bell pepper
1 T. chopped seeded jalapeño
  pepper
1/4 t. salt

1/4 t. black pepper
1/4 t. crushed red pepper
1 1/2 lbs. peeled & deveined
  shrimp
1 T. lime juice
1-14.5 oz. can no-salt-added diced
  tomatoes, drained

Heat the oil in a large non-stick skillet over medium-high heat. Add the bell pepper and jalapeño. Sauté 4 minutes. Add the salt, both peppers and shrimp. Cook 2 minutes. Stir in the lime juice and tomatoes and cook for 2 more minutes. Serve over the rice. Serve 4.

Nutritional Information: 324 Calories, 6.6 g Fat, 26.9 g Carbohydrate, 259 mg Cholesterol, 409 mg Sodium, 37.4 g Protein, 1.8 g Fiber.

SHRIMP SCAMPI

Robin Barbaree, Decatur, GA

4 t. olive oil
1 1/4 lbs. medium shrimp, peeled
  and deveined
6 garlic cloves, minced
1 C. low-sodium chicken broth

1/4 C. fresh lemon juice
1/4 C. + 1 T. finely-chopped fresh
  parsley
1/4 t. salt
1/4 t. black pepper

In a large non-stick skillet, heat the oil. Sauté the shrimp 2 to 3 minutes or until the shrimp turns pink. Add the garlic and cook, stirring constantly, about 30 seconds. With a slotted spoon, transfer the shrimp to a platter. Keep hot. In the skillet, combine the broth, lemon juice, 1/4 cup parsley, salt and pepper. Bring to a boil. Boil until the sauce is reduced by half. Spoon over the shrimp. Sprinkle with the remaining parsley. Serves 4.

Nutritional Information: 164 Calories, 6 g Fat, 3 g Carbohydrate, 210 mg Cholesterol, 24 g Protein, 0 gm Fiber.

I have PMS and ESP - That makes me a bitch who knows everything!

PECAN SHRIMP LINGUINE

8 oz. crimini mushrooms, sliced
3 qt. water
4 oz. spinach linguine, cooked
  according to directions, saving
  1/2 cup pasta water
2 t. olive oil
1/4 c. pecans, chopped coarsely

1 t. dried rosemary
8 oz. shrimp, peeled and deveined
2 T. flour
1/2 C. 2% milk
1/4 t. salt
Fresh black pepper

In a non-stick skillet over medium-high heat; add the mushrooms. Cook for 15 minutes, tossing frequently. Remove to a plate. In the skillet over medium-high heat, add the olive oil and pecans and cook, stirring frequently. Let the pecans brown, turn the heat down to medium. Add the rosemary and shrimp. Cook, tossing frequently, for about 5 minutes. Sprinkle the flour over the shrimp and toss until mixed. Cook for another 2 minutes. Add the milk and stir. Cook until the sauce begins to thicken. Add the pasta to the shrimp mixture and toss. If the sauce is too thick, add the pasta water. Serves 2.

Nutritional Information: 418 Calories, 18 g Fat, 32 g Carbohydrate, 175 mg Cholesterol, 503 mg Sodium, 33 g Protein, 5 g Fiber, 6 g Sugar.

Mirror, mirror on the wall, I am my mother after all.

SHRIMP FETTUCCINE WITH WINE SAUCE

12 oz. peeled and deveined shrimp
6 oz. spinach fettuccine, cooked
2 C. sliced fresh mushrooms
1 C. chopped onion
2 cloves garlic, minced
1 T. olive oil
1/4 C. dry white wine
1 T. fresh basil

1 1/2 t. fresh oregano
1 t. instant chicken bouillon
  granules
1 t. cornstarch
1/8 t. pepper
2 tomatoes, chopped
1/4 C. parsley
1/4 C. grated Parmesan cheese

While cooking the pasta, cook the mushrooms, onion and garlic in the olive oil until tender. Mix the wine, basil, oregano, granules, cornstarch and pepper together. Add to the mushroom mixture. Cook and stir until bubbly. Add the shrimp to the mixture. Cover and simmer about 3 minutes. Stir in the tomatoes and heat through. Drain the pasta and toss with the parsley. Spoon the shrimp mixture over the pasta. Sprinkle with the Parmesan cheese. Serves 4.

Nutritional Information: 390 Calories, 8 g Total Fat, 2 g Saturated Fat, 54 g Carbohydrate, 368 mg Sodium, 27 g Protein, 5 g Fiber, 8 Weight Watcher Points.

If you don't like the food, drink more wine.

SHRIMP JAMBALAYA

3/4 lb. uncooked shrimp, peeled
   and deveined
3/4 C. onion, finely chopped
1 clove garlic, minced
1 T. diet margarine
2 whole cloves
4 T. tomato paste
1/4 C. celery, finely chopped
1/8 C. green bell pepper, finely
   chopped

1/2 T. parsley
1-14 1/2 oz. can tomatoes,
   undrained
1/4 t. thyme
1/4 t. cayenne pepper
1/8 t. freshly-ground pepper
1/2 t. salt
3 C. cooked rice

Boil the shrimp until pink, about 5 minutes. Drain. Sauté the onion and garlic in the margarine for a few minutes. Add the tomatoes and tomato paste, stirring and cook for 5 minutes. Add all the ingredients, except the shrimp and rice. Cook 5 more minutes. Add all the ingredients, except the shrimp and rice. Cook 5 more minutes. Add the shrimp and rice. Stir over low heat until mixture is dry. Serve immediately. Serves 6.

Nutritional Information: 182 Calories, 2 g Fat, 33 g Carbohydrate, 43 mg Cholesterol, 391 mg Sodium, 10 g Protein, 2 g Dietary Fiber.

A woman is like a teabag. You never know
how strong she is until she gets into hot water.

LINGUINE WITH GRILLED SHRIMP

1 lb. medium shrimp, peeled and
   deveined
Salt and pepper, to taste
12 oz. linguine
1 T. extra-virgin olive oil
4 cloves garlic, minced

5 ripe tomatoes, coarsely chopped
1/4 C. chopped fresh basil
1/2 C. brine packed black olives,
   pitted and coarsely chopped
1/2 C. fresh grated Parmesan
   cheese

Place shrimp on skewers and sprinkle with the salt and pepper. Grill over a medium hot fire until just opaque throughout, about 3 to 4 minutes per side. Cut each shrimp into 3 pieces. Cook the linguine as directed on package. Heat the oil in a large skillet over medium heat and add the garlic. Cook just until garlic begins to brown and add tomatoes, black olives and shrimp. Mix in the basil and season with salt and pepper to taste. Serve over the cooked linguine and sprinkle with the cheese. Serves 6.

Nutritional Information: 377 Calories, 8 g Total Fat, 2 g Saturated Fat, 49 g Carbohydrate, 347 mg Sodium, 26 g Protein, 2.5 g Fiber, 8 Weight Watcher Points.

*Beware - the toe you step on today could be
connected to the ass you need to kiss tomorrow.*

TUNA BURGERS

2 T. nonfat mayonnaise
2 T. creamy mustard-mayonnaise
  blend
1 egg white
2-6 oz. cans albacore tuna in water,
  drained and flaked
1/2 C. dry bread crumbs, divided

1/4 C. chopped green onions
1/4 C. nonfat mayonnaise
4-1 1/2 oz. hamburger buns, split
4 lettuce leaves
4 slices tomatoes
4 slices sweet onion

Combine the first 3 ingredients in a bowl and stir well. Add the tuna, 1/4 cup bread crumbs and green onions. Mix well. Divide mixture into 4 equal parts and shape into patties. Press remaining bread crumbs evenly onto both ides of the patties. Coat a non-stick skillet with cooking spray and place over medium-high heat until hot. Add the patties, cover and cook 3 minutes. Turn patties over and cook 3 more minutes. Spread the mayonnaise on the buns. Place the patties and all other ingredients on the buns. Serves 4.

Nutritional Information: 335 Calories, 7.6 g Fat, 41.8 g Carbohydrate, 41 mg Cholesterol, 869 mg Sodium, 23.5 g Protein, 1.4 g Fiber.

Men are like chocolate - Wait too long
and only the weird nutty ones are left.

TUNA STEAKS WITH PINEAPPLE SAUCE

1 red onion, chopped
1-8 oz. can juice-packed crushed
  pineapple
3 garlic cloves, minced
3 T. ketchup
2 T. chopped green onions

1 t. cornstarch
1 t. brown sugar
1/2 t. salt
1/4 t. crushed red pepper
2 large tuna steaks

In a skillet saucepan, combine all the ingredients, except the tuna steaks. Bring to a boil over medium heat, stirring frequently. Cook, uncovered, 10 minutes, stirring occasionally. Reduce the heat to low and simmer, uncovered, 10 more minutes. Spray a broiler pan with non-stick spray. Cut the tuna steak in half to make 4 portions. Place the steaks on the broiler pan and top with the pineapple sauce. Broil for 12 minutes. Serves 4.

Nutritional Information: 307 Calories, 8 g Fat, 64 mg Cholesterol, 453 mg Sodium.

May all your wrinkles be laugh lines.

TUNA CAKES WITH LEMON DILL SAUCE

1-12 oz. can white tuna packed in
    water, drained
3/4 C. seasoned bread crumbs
1/4 C. minced green onion
2 T. chopped drained pimentos
1 egg

1/2 C. skim milk
1/2 t. grated lemon peel
2 T. low-fat margarine
1/4 C. nonfat chicken broth
1 T. lemon juice
1/4 t. dried dill weed

Combine the first 7 ingredients. Make 8 patties. In a large skillet, melt the margarine. Cook the patties until golden brown on both sides. For the sauce, heat the broth, lemon juice and dill until warm. Spoon over each patty. Serves 4.

Nutritional Information: 265 Calories, 8 g Total Fat, 2 g Saturated Fat, 19 g Carbohydrate, 1046 mg Sodium, 29 g Protein, 0 g Fiber, 6 Weight Watcher Points.

GRILLED TUNA TERIYAKI

2 T. light soy sauce
1 T. Chinese rice wine
1 large clove garlic, minced

1 T. minced fresh ginger root
4-6 oz. tuna steaks
1 T. vegetable oil

In a shallow dish, stir together the soy sauce, rice wine, garlic and ginger. Place the tuna in the marinade and turn to coat. Cover and refrigerate for at least 30 minutes or longer. Preheat grill for medium-high heat. Brush both sides of the steaks with the oil. Cook tuna for 3 to 5 minutes per side. Serves 4.

Nutritional Information: 227 Calories, 5.1 g Total Fat, 1.5 g Total Carbohydrate, 77 mg Cholesterol, 329 mg Sodium, 40.4 g Protein, 0.1 g Dietary Fiber.

SOUTHWESTERN SALMON

1 1/2 C. fresh cilantro leaves
1 T. fresh lime juice
1/2 t. ground cumin
1/4 t. salt
Dash hot red pepper sauce
1/4 C. water

1/2 lb. salmon steak
1 yellow bell pepper, seeded and
   sliced
1 red bell pepper, seeded and
   sliced

When ready to cook, preheat the oven to 400 degrees F. In a food processor, place the first 6 ingredients. Purée. Transfer to a large zip-close plastic bag. Add the salmon. Seal the bag and coat the salmon. Refrigerate, turning the bag occasionally, 1 hour. Spray a 9-inch square baking dish with non-stick spray. Arrange the bell peppers in a single layer in the pan. Bake, turning once, 20 minutes. Drain the salmon and discard the marinade. Place the salmon on top of the peppers. Bake for 5 to 6 minutes. Serves 2.

Nutritional Information: 236 Calories, 12 g Fat, 7 g Carbohydrate, 75 mg Cholesterol, 198 mg Sodium, 24 g Protein, 1 g Fiber.

I understand the concepts of cooking and
cleaning, just not how they apply to me!

SALMON CROQUETTES

1-15 1/2 oz. can salmon, drained
  and flaked
2 T. onion, grated
4 egg whites, beaten until frothy
  and divided

1/8 t. pepper
1/4 t. salt
1/2 C. bread crumbs

Preheat oven to 350 degrees F. Place the salmon in a colander and drain for 1 minute. Combine the salmon, onion, 2 egg whites, salt and pepper and half of the bread crumbs. Stir well. Divide mixture in 6 equal portions. Dip each croquette in the remaining egg white mixture, then in the remaining bread crumbs. Bake for 25 to 30 minutes, or until crust is brown. Serves 6.

Nutritional Information: 148 Calories, 5 g Fat, 6 g Carbohydrate, 31 mg Cholesterol, 551 mg Sodium, 17 g Protein, 0 g Dietary Fiber.

I'm still a hot Babe, but now it comes in flashes!

PAN-SEARED SALMON
WITH BABY ARUGULA SALAD

2-6 oz. fillets of salmon
1 1/2 T. fresh lemon juice

1 1/2 T. olive oil
Salt and pepper, to taste

Place the salmon fillets in a shallow bowl. Toss well with the lemon juice, olive oil, salt and pepper. Let marinate for 15 minutes. Spray a skillet with Pam. Cook the salmon, skin-side down over medium-high heat for 2 to 3 minutes. Reduce the heat to medium. Cover the pan and cook until the salmon is cooked through, 3 to 4 more minutes.

Salad:
3 C. baby arugula leaves
2/3 C. cherry tomatoes, halved
1/4 C. thinly-slivered red onion

1 T. extra-virgin olive oil
1 T. red wine vinegar

Combine the first 3 ingredients. Drizzle with the oil and vinegar. Serves 2.

Nutritional Information: 390 Calories, 23 g Fat, 4 g Carbohydrate, 105 mg Cholesterol, 40 g Protein.

I'm out of estrogen, and I have a gun.

BARBEQUE ROASTED SALMON

1/4 C. pineapple juice
2 T. fresh lemon juice
4-6 oz. salmon fillets
2 T. brown sugar

1/2 t. chipotle powder
2 t. grated lemon rind
1/2 t. salt
1/2 t. ground cinnamon

Preheat oven to 400 degrees F. when ready to bake. Combine first 3 ingredients in a zip-top plastic bag. Seal and refrigerate for 1 hour, turning occasionally. Remove fish from the bag and discard the marinade. Combine the sugar and next 5 ingredients in a bowl. Rub over fish. Place in an 11x7-inch baking pan coated with cooking spray. Bake 12 minutes. Serves 4.

Nutritional Information: 314 Calories, 14 g Total Fat, 2.5 g Saturated Fat, 9 g Carbohydrate, 405 mg Sodium, 35 g Protein, 1 g Fiber, 7 Weight Watcher Points.

A successful man is one who makes more money than his wife can spend. A successful woman is one who can find such a man.

ROAST SALMON WITH LIME SALSA

2 large limes
1/3 C. very thinly-sliced red onion
1 1/2 T. chopped cilantro leaves
1 small jalapeño pepper, halved,
   seeded and very thinly sliced

Pinch of sugar
2 T. olive oil, divided
4-6 oz. salmon fillets

Preheat oven to 425 degrees F. Carefully peel the limes. Cut in between the membranes to release the lime section into a bowl. Cut each section crosswise into quarters. Stir in the onion, cilantro and jalapeño into the bowl with the lime. Add 1 tablespoon of olive oil, sugar and salt. Toss well. Heat an ovenproof skillet over medium-high heat until it begins to smoke and add the 1 tablespoon olive oil. Season the salmon on both sides with salt and pepper. Place in the skillet. Sear until nicely browned, about 1 minute per side. Place in the oven. Roast for 4 to 6 minutes. Serve with the lime salsa. Serves 4.

Nutritional Information: 307 Calories, 18.3 g Fat, 8.1 Weight Watcher Points.

Go braless, it pulls the wrinkles out of your face.

CRAB AND ASPARAGUS CASSEROLE

1-10 oz. pkg. frozen cut asparagus
1 C. sliced fresh mushrooms
1/4 C. finely-chopped onion
1 T. margarine
1 T. cornstarch
1/4 t. salt

1/8 t. ground nutmeg
1 C. skim milk
8 oz. fresh or frozen crabmeat
2 T. chopped toasted almonds
2 T. grated Parmesan cheese

Preheat oven to 400 degrees F. Cook asparagus according to package directions. Drain well and set aside. In a medium saucepan, cook mushrooms and onion in the margarine until onion is tender. Stir in cornstarch, salt and nutmeg. Stir in the milk all at once. Cook and stir until thickened and bubbly. Cook and stir for 1 more minute. Stir in the crab and asparagus. Spoon mixture into a casserole dish. In a bowl, stir the almonds and cheese together. Sprinkle atop the casserole. Bake for 10 minutes. Serves 4.

Nutritional Information: 174 Calories, 7 g Total Fat, 1 g Saturated Fat, 10 g Carbohydrate, 441 mg Sodium, 18 g Protein, 2 g Fiber, 4 Weight Watcher Points.

How naughty can I be and still go to heaven?

CRAB CAKES

6 oz. crabmeat
2 hard-boiled eggs, whites only, chopped
1 oz. reduced-fat potato chips, crushed
2 T. chopped onion

4 T. nonfat sour cream
1 T. fresh parsley, chopped
1/2 t. coriander seed
2 T. light mayonnaise
1 t. grated lemon peel
1 T. cilantro

Mix all ingredients. Make 8 patties. Coat the pan with nonfat cooking spray. Place crab cakes into pan and sauté until side is golden brown. Turn cakes over and cook until golden brown. Serves 8.

Nutritional Information: 70 Calories, 2 g Fat, 0 g Saturated Fat, 9 g Carbohydrate, 0 mg Cholesterol, 180 mg Sodium, 4 g Protein, 1 g Fiber, 4 g Sugar.

RED SNAPPER WITH MANGO SALSA

1 firm-ripe mango, peeled, pitted and finely chopped
1/2 red onion, chopped fine, soaked in cold water for 20 minutes and drained
1 jalapeño, minced

3 T. fresh lime juice
2 T. chopped fresh basil
Salt and pepper, to taste
4 t. vegetable oil
4-6 oz. red snapper fillets, skinned
Juice of half a lemon

In a bowl, mix the first 6 ingredients. Chill for 1 hour. In a large non-stick skillet, heat the oil over medium-high heat. Add the fish and sauté for 3 to 4 minutes a side. Sprinkle with the lemon juice. Top with the salsa. Serves 4.

Nutritional Information: 258 Calories, 7 g Fat, 77 mg Sodium.

OREGANO SNAPPER

4 snapper fillets
1 t. dried oregano
1/2 t. ground cumin
1/4 t. salt

1/4 t. pepper
Paprika, to taste
1/2 a lemon

Preheat oven to 350 degrees F. Line a baking pan with foil. Lightly spray with vegetable oil spray. Place the fish on the pan. Sprinkle the fish with all the ingredients, except the lemon. Lightly spray with the vegetable oil spray. Bake for 10 to 12 minutes. Squeeze the lemon over the fish. Serves 4.

Nutritional Information: 114 Calories, 1.5 g Fat, 1 g Carbohydrate, 40 mg Cholesterol, 195 mg Sodium, 23 g Protein.

OVEN-FRIED FISH

Robin Mantia, Marble Falls, TX

1 T. + 1 1/2 t. corn oil stick
  margarine, melted
1 T. fresh lime juice
1/2 t. dried basil, crumbled
1/4 t. salt
1/4 t. pepper

1/4 t. paprika
1/8 t. garlic powder
11 fat-free, low-sodium saltine
  crackers, crushed
4 flounder fillets

Preheat oven to 475 degrees F. Lightly spray a non-stick baking sheet with vegetable oil spray. In a bowl, add the first 7 ingredients. Put the cracker crumbs in another bowl. Dip the fish in the margarine mixture, then roll it in the cracker crumbs. Arrange the fish in a single layer on a baking sheet. Spoon the remaining margarine mixture over the fish. Bake 15 minutes. Serves 4.

Nutritional Information: 165 Calories, 5.5 g Fat, 8 g Carbohydrate, 52 mg Cholesterol, 327 mg Sodium, 20 g Protein.

CRISPY FISH STICKS

3-1 oz. slices French bread, cubed
3 T. reduced-fat mayonnaise
2 t. water
1/2 t. grated lemon rind

1 t. lemon juice
1 1/2 lbs. white fish fillets, cut into
1-inch-wide strips

Preheat oven to 350 degrees F. Add the bread cubes to a blender. Process 30 seconds. Sprinkle the crumbs on an ungreased baking sheet. Bake for 12 minutes. Set aside. Reset the oven to 425 degrees F. Combine the next 4 ingredients in a shallow bowl. Dip fish in the mayonnaise mixture and then dredge in the bread crumbs. Place fish on a baking sheet coated with a cooking spray. Bake for 22 to 25 minutes. Serves 6.

Nutritional Information: 167 Calories, 3.6 g Fat, 8.4 g Carbohydrate, 45 mg Cholesterol, 109 mg Sodium, 23.3 g Protein, 0.3 g Fiber.

FISH STEW

1 1/2 t. instant beef bouillon
1 1/2 C. water
1 t. chopped garlic
1 T. catsup
1 onion, sliced

1 C. sliced carrots
1-16 oz. can green beans, drained
1 lb. fish fillet
1/2 t. dried basil

In a skillet, add the first 4 ingredients. Add the vegetables and top with the fish and basil. Bring to a boil. Reduce the heat and simmer, covered, for 10 minutes. Serves 4.

Nutritional Information: 170 Calories, 2 g Fat.

FISH BURRITOS

4 flour tortillas
1/3 C. yellow cornmeal
1/2 t. salt

1 lb. lean fish fillets, cut into
   1-inch pieces
1 T. vegetable oil
1/2 C. green sauce

Preheat oven to 300 degrees F. Wrap tortillas in foil. Heat in the oven for 15 minutes. Mix the cornmeal and salt in a bowl. Coat the fish with the cornmeal. Heat the oil in a skillet and cook fish for 6 to 7 minutes on medium-high heat. Turn occasionally. Divide the fish among the tortillas. Top each with 2 tablespoons of the green sauce. Roll up tortillas. Serves 4.

Nutritional Information: 225 Calories, 7 g Fat, 14 g Carbohydrate, 35 mg Cholesterol, 450 mg Sodium, 25 g Protein.

GRILLED SWORDFISH

4 T. reduced-sodium soy sauce
2 garlic cloves, minced
2 t. sugar

4 t. fresh lemon juice
1/4 t. crusted red pepper
6-6 oz. swordfish steaks

In a bowl, whisk the first 5 ingredients together. Arrange the fish in one layer in a shallow dish and pour the marinade over it. Chill, covered, for 30 minutes. Remove the fish from the marinade and pat it dry. Grill on a rack sprayed with non-stick vegetable oil spray 4 inches from the heat. Cook for 3 to 4 minutes per side. Serves 6.

Nutritional Information: 208 Calories, 7 g Fat, 109 mg Sodium.

GRILLED FISH WITH CORN TOMATO SALSA

1 ear of corn, husked
2 ripe tomatoes, chopped
2 T. fresh lime juice
2 T. cider vinegar

2 T. chopped fresh cilantro
2 T. green chili pepper, chopped
Salt and pepper, to taste
4 orange roughy fillets

Cook the corn in boiling water for 30 seconds. Cool under running cold water. Cut off the kernels. Combine all the ingredients, except the fish. Chill. Spray a grill with non-stick spray. Spray the fillets with the spray. Grill each side for a few minutes, just until the fish flakes. Serve with the salsa. Serves 4.

Nutritional Information: 188 Calories, 8 g Total Fat, 0 g Saturated Fat, 11 g Carbohydrate, 80 mg Sodium, 18 g Protein, 1.5 g Fiber, 4 Weight Watcher Points.

CREOLE CATFISH FILLETS

2 T. minced onion
3 T. plain low-fat yogurt
1 1/2 T. nonfat mayonnaise
1 1/2 T. Dijon mustard
1 T. reduced-calorie ketchup
1/2 t. dried thyme
1/4 t. grated lemon rind

1/8 t. ground red pepper
1 t. paprika
1/2 t. onion powder
1/8 t. salt
1/8 t. ground red pepper
1-4 oz. catfish fillets

Combine the first 8 ingredients, stirring well. Cover and chill. Combine the next 4 ingredients and stir well. Rub the mixture over both sides of fish. Arrange the fish in a wire grilling basket coated with cooking spray. Place on the grill and cook 6 minutes on each side. Serve with sauce. Serves 4.

Nutritional Information: 178 Calories, 6 g Fat, 14.8 g Carbohydrate, 66 mg Cholesterol, 372 mg Sodium, 22.7 g Protein, 0.7 g Fiber.

EGGPLANT PARMESAN

Gary Gardia, St. George, UT

2 medium eggplants, peeled and cut crosswise into 1/2-inch slices
4 egg whites, lightly beaten
1/2 C. unseasoned dry bread crumbs
1/2 t. dried basil
1/2 t. dried oregano
1/2 t. garlic powder
1/4 t. ground black pepper
3 C. reduced-sodium tomato sauce
2 C. shredded reduced-fat Mozzarella cheese
1/4 C. grated reduced-fat Parmesan cheese
2 T. chopped fresh parsley

Preheat the broiler. Coat a non-stick baking sheet with a cooking spray. Place the egg whites in a shallow bowl. In another shallow bowl, mix the bread crumbs, basil, oregano, garlic powder and pepper. Dip each eggplant slice first into the egg whites, then into the crumb mixture. Place the eggplant on the baking sheet. Broil for 5 minutes per side. Spread about 1/2 cup of the tomato sauce in the bottom of a 9x13x2-inch baking dish. Arrange a layer of eggplant on top of the sauce. Sprinkle with 1/2 cup of the Mozzarella cheese and 1 tablespoon of the Parmesan cheese. Repeat the layers ending with the tomato sauce. Sprinkle with the parsley and cover with foil. Set the oven on 350 degrees F. and bake for 30 minutes. Serves 4.

Nutritional Information: 408.5 Calories, 16.5 g Fat, 42.1 g Carbohydrate, 249 mg Cholesterol, 707.5 mg Sodium, 30.5 g Protein, 11.4 g Fiber, 6.7 g Total Sugars.

EGGPLANT CHEESE QUESADILLAS

1 C. finely-cubed peeled eggplant
1/2 C. diced tomatoes
1/3 C. chopped green onions
1/4 C. apple juice

1 C. shredded low-fat Monterey
Jack cheese
1/2 C. nonfat sour cream
1/4 C. grated Parmesan cheese
8-10-inch low-fat flour tortillas

In a non-stick skillet over medium-high heat, combine the first 4 ingredients. Cover and cook for 3 minutes. Uncover, cook and stir for 5 minutes. Transfer to a plate. In a small bowl, combine the next 3 ingredients. Mix well. Spread on 4 tortillas. Top with the vegetables. Cover each with another tortilla. In a clean skillet, brown each quesadilla for 1 minute on each side. Cut into wedges. Serves 4.

Nutritional Information: 345.2 Calories, 12.6 g Fat, 42.4 g Carbohydrate, 27.3 mg Cholesterol, 885.2 mg Sodium, 14.5 g Protein, 2.2 g Fiber, 4.3 g Total Sugars.

I can only please one person per day. Today is not your day. Tomorrow isn't looking too good either.

VEGETARIAN LASAGNA PIE

2 T. olive oil
3 carrots, finely chopped
1 zucchini, finely chopped
1 red pepper, finely chopped
4 garlic cloves, minced
3 C. fresh mushrooms, sliced
2-6 oz. pkg. baby spinach
2 T. snipped fresh basil
1 beaten egg

1-15 oz. carton low-fat ricotta
  cheese
1/3 C. shredded Parmesan cheese
Salt and pepper, to taste
1-26 oz. jar tomato and basil pasta
  sauce
14 dried lasagna noodles, cooked
  according to pkg. directions
2 C. shredded low-fat Mozzarella
  cheese

Preheat oven to 375 degrees F. In a large skillet, add 1 tablespoon of the oil. Heat over medium-high heat. Add the carrots, zucchini, red pepper and half of the garlic. Cook and stir for about 5 minutes. Place in a bowl. Heat the remaining oil in the same skillet. Add the mushrooms and remaining garlic. Cook and stir about 5 minutes. Gradually add the spinach. Cook and stir for 1 to 2 minutes, or until the spinach is wilted. Using a slotted spoon, transfer spinach mixture to another bowl. Stir in the basil. In a bowl, combine the egg, ricotta cheese, Parmesan cheese, salt and pepper. Spread 1/2 cup to the pasta sauce in the bottom of a 9-inch springform pan. Arrange 3 or 4 lasagna noodles over the sauce. Trim any overlapping as necessary to cover the sauce. Top with half spinach mixture. Top with half of the ricotta mixture. Top with another layer of noodles. Spread with half of the remaining pasta sauce. Top with all of the zucchini mixture. Sprinkle with half of the Mozzarella cheese. Top with another layer of noodles. Layer with remaining spinach mixture and ricotta mixture. Top with another layer of noodles and remaining sauce. Gently press down pie with back of spatula. Place the pan on a foil-lined baking sheet. Bake for about 1 hour. Top with Mozzarella cheese for the last 15 minutes. Cover and let stand on a wire rack for 15 minutes before serving. Carefully remove side of the springform pan. Serves 8.

Nutritional Information: 240 Calories, 6.2 g Fat, 36.9 g Carbohydrate, 30 mg Cholesterol, 128 mg Sodium, 10.4 g Protein, 3.7 g Fiber, 3.5 g Sugar, 577 mg Potassium.

MACARONI AND CHEESE

2 C. dry macaroni, cooked
  according to directions
1/2 C. chopped onion
1/2 C. evaporated skim milk

1 egg, beaten
1/4 t. black pepper
1 1/4 C. low-fat sharp Cheddar
  cheese, finely shredded

Preheat oven to 350 degrees F. Spray a casserole dish with non-stick spray. Lightly spray a saucepan with non-stick spray. Add the onions and sauté for 3 minutes. In a bowl, add the macaroni, onion and rest of the ingredients and mix thoroughly. Place in the casserole dish. Bake for 25 minutes. Let stand 10 minutes before serving. Serves 8.

Nutritional Information: 200 Calories, 4 g Fat, 34 mg Cholesterol, 120 mg Sodium.

PASTA WITH SWISS CHARD AND CHEESE

Gary Gardia, St. George, UT

2 t. olive oil
1 T. chopped onion
2 garlic cloves, minced
1 C. Swiss chard, washed, drained
  and chopped

Dash of crushed red pepper
1/4 C. low-sodium, low-fat chicken
  broth
1 1/2 C. cooked spaghetti
2 t. grated Parmesan cheese

In a non-stick skillet, heat the oil. Add the onion and garlic and cook over medium-high heat, stirring frequently, about 1 minute. Add the chard and red pepper. Reduce the heat to medium and cook, stirring frequently, for 2 minutes. Add the broth and reduce the heat to low and let simmer for 8 minutes. Add the spaghetti and toss. Sprinkle with the cheese. Serves 2.

Nutritional Information: 200 Calories, 5 g Fat, 32 g Carbohydrate, 0 mg Cholesterol, 47 mg Sodium, 6 g Protein, 22 mg Calcium.

PASTA PRIMAVERA

Olive oil
2 small zucchini, cut into 1 1/2-
  inch chunks
3 1/2 t. salt, less if need be
1 eggplant, cut into 1-inch pieces
1 onion, diced
2 yellow peppers, cut into 1-inch
  pieces

1-14.5 oz. can stewed tomatoes
1/2 t. black pepper
1/2 t. dried basil leaves
1/2 t. sugar
12 oz. corkscrew or penne pasta,
  cooked according to directions
1/4 C. grated Parmesan cheese

In a non-stick skillet over medium-high heat, add 1 tablespoon olive oil. Add the zucchini and 1/4 teaspoon salt until the zucchini is tender-crisp. Remove and place in a bowl. Add 1 tablespoon of olive oil in the same skillet, add the eggplant, onion and 1/2 teaspoon salt, stirring occasionally, until eggplant begins to brown slightly. Add the yellow pepper and 1 tablespoon oil and cook, stirring occasionally, until the vegetables are golden. Stir in the tomatoes, pepper, basil, sugar and 3/4 teaspoon salt. Heat to boiling and reduce heat to low. Cover and simmer 15 minutes, stirring occasionally, until the vegetables are tender. Stir in the zucchini and heat. Pour over the cooked pasta and mix with the Parmesan cheese. Serves 4.

Nutritional Information: 540 Calories, 14 g Fat, 0 g Carbohydrate, 4 mg Cholesterol, 1280 mg Sodium.

FETTUCCINE ALFREDO

8 oz. dry fettuccine pasta, cooked
   according to directions
1 T. olive oil
1 C. evaporated skim milk
1/3 C. grated Parmesan cheese

1/2 t. dried basil
1 1/2 lemons, juiced
1 pinch ground pepper
Fresh basil

After draining the pasta return to pan. Add the olive oil, toss to coat. Add the rest of the ingredients, except the fresh basil, and cook over medium-high until bubbly, stirring constantly. Top with additional Parmesan cheese and fresh basil. Serves 4.

Nutritional Information: 290 Calories, 4.9 g Fat, 53.6 g Carbohydrate, 3 mg Cholesterol, 78 mg Sodium, 12.8 g Protein, 3.9 g Fiber.

Dull women have immaculate homes.

FRIED RICE WITH PINEAPPLE AND TOFU

Grace Qualls, Lafayette, LA

1-14 oz. pkg. firm tofu, drained and cut into 1/2-inch cubes
2 T. roasted peanuts or peanut oil, divided
1/4 t. salt
1 C. red bell pepper, chopped
3/4 C. thinly-sliced green onions
1 C. shelled green peas
1/4 lb. snow peas, trimmed and cut lengthwise into thin strips

4 C. cooked long-grain brown rice, chilled
1/4 C. chopped fresh cilantro, divided
1-15 1/4 oz. can pineapple chunks in juice, drained
1/4 C. low-sodium soy sauce
1 T. chopped unsalted dry-roasted peanuts

Place tofu between paper towels until barely moist. Heat 1 tablespoon oil in a large non-stick skillet over medium-high heat. Add tofu and cook 8 minutes, or until golden. Sprinkle with salt. Remove the tofu from the pan. Heat 1 tablespoon oil in pan over medium-high heat. Add the bell pepper and onions. Sauté 2 minutes. Add the peas and sauté 30 seconds. Stir in the rice and cook 2 minutes. Add tofu, 2 tablespoons cilantro and pineapple. Cook 1 minute, stirring gently. Remove from the heat. Stir in the soy sauce and peanuts. Sprinkle with 2 tablespoons cilantro. Serves 7.

Nutritional Information: 256 Calories, 8.5 g Fat, 36.5 g Carbohydrate, 0 mg Cholesterol, 375 mg Sodium, 10.3 g Protein.

SPICY RICE WITH BLACK-EYED PEAS

1-10 oz. pkg. frozen black-eyed
 peas, cooked as pkg. directions
3/4 C. uncooked instant rice
1/2 C. chopped onions
1/4 C. chopped red bell pepper
1 T. chopped fresh oregano

1/4 t. salt
1/8 t. cayenne red pepper
1 clove garlic, finely chopped
1-16 oz. can whole tomatoes,
 undrained

In a skillet add the cooked peas and remaining ingredients. Heat to boiling and reduce heat. Cover and simmer about 10 minutes. Serves 4.

Nutritional Information: 215 Calories, 1 g Fat, 44 g Carbohydrate, 0 mg Cholesterol, 610 mg Sodium, 9 g Protein.

Blessed are the flexible, for they shall never be bent out of shape.

NOTES & RECIPES

VEGETABLES

NOTES

BAKED STUFFED POTATOES

4 medium baking potatoes
3/4 C. low-fat cottage cheese
1/4 C. low-fat 1% milk
2 T. soft margarine

1 t. dill weed
3/4 t. herb seasoning
4 drops hot pepper sauce
2 t. grated Parmesan cheese

Preheat oven to 425 degrees F. Prick potatoes with a fork. Bake for 60 minutes. Cut potatoes in half lengthwise. Carefully scoop out potato leaving about 1/2 inch of pulp inside shell. Mash pulp in a large bowl. Mix, by hand, remaining ingredients, except the cheese. Spoon mixture into the shells. Sprinkle top with the cheese. Place on a baking sheet and return to oven. Bake 15 to 20 minutes, or until tops are golden brown. Serves 8.

Nutritional Information: 113 Calories, 3 g Fat, 1 mg Cholesterol, 136 mg Sodium.

GARLIC MASHED POTATOES

Carol Adams, Fort Stockton, TX

1 lb. potatoes, peeled and
  quartered
2 C. skim milk

2 large cloves garlic, chopped
1/2 t. white pepper

Cook potatoes, covered, in a small amount of boiling water for 20 to 25 minutes, or until tender. Remove from heat. Drain. In a small saucepan over low heat, cook the garlic in milk until garlic is soft, about 30 minutes. Add to the potatoes. Stir in the pepper. Beat with an electric mixer on low speed. Makes 4 servings.

Nutritional Information: 141 Calories, 1 g Fat, 2 mg Cholesterol, 70 mg Sodium.

CHIPOTLE MASHED POTATOES

2 lb. medium red potatoes, cut into
  chunks
6 T. margarine

1/2 C. chipotle salsa
1/4 C. fresh cilantro, chopped
Salt and pepper, to taste

Place potatoes in a large saucepan with water to cover. Bring to a boil, reduce heat to medium-low and cook until potatoes are tender, about 20 minutes. Drain and return to the pot. Set the pot over low heat, add the rest of the ingredients. Mash. Serves 6.

Nutritional Information: 135 Calories, 1 g Fat, 2 mg Cholesterol, 70 mg Sodium.

POTATO CASSEROLE

2 lb. pkg. frozen hash brown
  potatoes
1 C. whipped low-fat butter,
  melted
2 C. fat-free sour cream
1/2 C. onion, finely chopped
1-10 3/4 oz. can low-fat cream of
  chicken soup

4 oz. low-fat sharp Cheddar
  cheese, grated
1/2 t. salt
1/2 t. pepper
3 3/4 C. corn flakes, crushed
1 T. butter, melted

Preheat oven to 350° degrees F. Coat a 2-quart casserole dish with non-stick spray. Combine the first 8 ingredients and mix well. Pour into casserole dish. Combine the corn flake crumbs with the melted butter and spread over potatoes. Bake for 45 minutes. Serves 8.

Nutritional Information: 332 Calories, 12 g Fat, 43 g Carbohydrate, 44 mg Cholesterol, 718 mg Sodium, 11 g Protein, 2 g Fiber.

ROASTED POTATOES

1 1/2 lb. unpeeled new potatoes,
  cut into halves
1/2 head garlic, whole cloves

1/4 C. chopped fresh rosemary
Salt and pepper, to taste

Preheat oven to 375 degrees F. Place the potatoes into a baking pan with the whole cloves of garlic and small amount of water. Toss with the rosemary. Cover pan and bake for 20 minutes, then remove the cover and roast for another 10 to 15 minutes. Add salt and pepper to taste. Serves 3.

Nutritional Information: 224 Calories, 0.5 g Fat.

CHEESY SCALLOPED POTATOES

Gary Gardia, St. George, UT

1/2 C. chopped onion
1 clove garlic, minced
2 T. flour
1/2 t. salt
1/8 t. pepper

1 1/2 C. skim milk
4 medium red potatoes, peeled
  and thinly sliced
1/2 C. shredded reduced-fat
  Cheddar cheese

Preheat oven to 350 degrees F. Spray a small saucepan with non-stick coating. Preheat over medium heat. Add the onion and garlic. Cook and stir until onion is tender. In a small bowl, combine the flour, salt and pepper. Gradually stir milk into flour mixture until smooth. Add to the saucepan. Cook and stir over medium heat until thickened and bubbly. Spray a 1 1/2-quart casserole with non-stick coating. Place half to the potatoes in the casserole. Top with half of the sauce. Repeat. Bake, covered, for 40 minutes. Uncover and bake about 30 minutes. Remove and sprinkle with the cheese. Let stand for 10 minutes before serving. Serves 8.

Nutritional Information: 114 Calories, 2 g Fat, 20 g Carbohydrate, 6 mg Cholesterol, 211 mg Sodium, 5 g Protein, 1 g Fiber.

CRANBERRY SWEET POTATOES

3/4 C. orange juice
2 sweet potatoes, cut in half, then
  lengthwise into 8 wedges
1 t. extra-virgin olive oil

1/2 t. cinnamon
1 t. honey
1/2 t. cumin
1/4 C. dried cranberries

Preheat oven to 400 degrees F. Mix the orange juice, olive oil, cinnamon, cumin, honey and salt. Toss with the potatoes. Spread into a shallow baking dish. Bake, covered, for 45 minutes, basting once or twice. Uncover and bake for 15 minutes, then sprinkle with the cranberries.

Nutritional Information: 104 Calories, 1 g Fat, 32 g Carbohydrate, 10 mg Sodium, 1.5 g Protein, 2.3 g Fiber.

OVEN-FRIED POTATOES

2 russet potatoes, unpeeled
1 egg white

1 t. Cajun seasoning
Salt and pepper, to taste

Preheat oven to 450 degrees F. Spray a baking sheet with non-stick cooking spray. Wash potatoes and cut lengthwise into 8 wedges. In a bowl, mix the egg white and seasonings. Add the potatoes and coat. Spread the potatoes on the baking sheet. Spray the tops of the potatoes with the non-stick cooking spray. Bake for 25 to 30 minutes, turning potatoes once. Serves 4.

Nutritional Information: 73 Calories, 0.1 g Fat.

ORANGE SWEET POTATOES

1 T. butter
3 large sweet potatoes, peeled and
  cut in half lengthwise, then into
  1/2-inch slices
1 C. orange juice

1 t. grated orange peel
2/3 t. salt
1/2 t. grated nutmeg
1/4 t. black pepper
1/4 C. packed brown sugar

Preheat oven to 375 degrees F. Coat a 9x9-inch baking dish with non-stick spray. Brown butter in a small skillet over medium heat, swirling the skillet, until butter turns a pretty color. Remove and set aside. Place potato slices into the baking dish. Pour orange juice over the potatoes. Sprinkle with the orange peel, salt, nutmeg and pepper. Top with brown sugar and browned butter. Cover and bake for 40 to 45 minutes. Serves 4.

Nutritional Information: 185 Calories, 3 g Fat, 39 g Carbohydrate, 8 mg Cholesterol, 442 mg Sodium, 2 g Protein, 3 g Fiber.

Crazy is a relative term in this family.

SWEET POTATO PIE

1 1/4 C. flour
1/4 t. sugar
1/3 C. skim milk
2 T. vegetable oil
1/4 C. white sugar
1/4 C. brown sugar
1/2 t. salt

1/4 t. nutmeg
3 eggs, beaten
1/4 C. evaporated skim milk
1 t. vanilla extract
3 C. sweet potatoes, cooked and
  mashed

Preheat oven to 350° degrees F. Combine the flour and sugar in a bowl. Add the milk and oil to the flour mixture. Stir with a fork until well mixed, then form pastry into a smooth ball with your hands. Roll the ball between two 12-inch squares of waxed paper. Roll out. Place the crust into a pie plate. In a bowl, mix the rest of the ingredients in the order given. Pour into pie shell. Bake 60 minutes. Cool and cut into 16 slices. Serving size 1 slice.

Nutritional Information: 147 Calories, 3 g Fat, 40 mg Cholesterol, 98 mg Sodium.

ROASTED GARLIC LEMON BROCCOLI

2 heads broccoli, separated into
  florets
2 t. extra-virgin olive oil
1 t. sea salt

1/2 t. pepper
1 clove garlic, minced
1/2 t. lemon juice

Preheat oven to 400 degrees F. In a large bowl, add the oil, sea salt, pepper and garlic. Toss the broccoli in the mixture. Place on baking sheet and bake for 15 to 20 minutes. Place broccoli on serving plate and squeeze the lemon on top. Serves 6.

Nutritional Information: 49 Calories, 1.9 g Fat, 7 g Carbohydrate, 0 mg Cholesterol, 417 mg Sodium, 2.9 g Protein, 2.7 g Fiber.

BROCCOLI WITH GARLIC AND PINE NUTS

5 C. broccoli florets
3 T. olive oil
6 cloves garlic

1/4 C. hazelnuts
Kosher salt, to taste

Place the broccoli in a Ziploc bag, seal and poke holes in the bag to allow steam to escape. Microwave. Heat the olive oil over medium heat in a frying pan. Chop garlic finely. Add the pine nuts, stirring to toast lightly, about 1 to 2 minutes. Turn heat down, add garlic, and heat until garlic is browned. Add the broccoli to the pan. Coat with the oil mixture and cook another 2 to 3 minutes. Salt to taste. Serves 5.

Nutritional Information: 152 Calories, 13 g Fat, 8 g Carbohydrate, 0 mg Cholesterol, 147 mg Sodium.

BROCCOLI AND RICE CASSEROLE

1 C. instant rice, uncooked
1/2 C. onion, chopped
1/4 C. nonfat milk
4 oz. light Velveeta cheese, diced
2 T. butter, softened

2-10 oz. pkg. frozen chopped broccoli, thawed and drained
1-10 3/4 oz. reduced-fat reduced-sodium condensed cream of mushroom soup

Preheat oven to 350° degrees F. Mix all the ingredients together. Place in a 2-quart casserole dish. Bake for 45 minutes. Serves 6.

Nutritional Information: 127 Calories, 4.3 g Fat, 19.4 g Carbohydrate, 10 mg Cholesterol, 57 mg Sodium, 4.4 g Protein.

BROCCOLI CASSEROLE

1 1/2 C. shredded nonfat Cheddar
  cheese
1 3/4 C. nonfat cottage cheese
1/3 C. fat-free egg substitute
1/3 C. finely-chopped onion

2-10 oz. pkg. frozen chopped
  broccoli, thawed and drained
2 t. flour
1/4 t. white pepper
3 T. finely-ground fat-free whole
  wheat cracker crumbs

Preheat oven to 350 degrees F. Set aside 1/2 cup of the cheese. Combine the rest of the cheese and all the remaining ingredients, except the crumbs, in a large bowl. Mix well. Coat a 2 1/2-quart casserole dish with non-stick cooking spray. Place the broccoli mixture in the dish, sprinkle with the crumbs and spread the remaining cheese over the top. Bake for 50 minutes. Let set for 5 minutes before serving. Serves 12.

Nutritional Information: 196 Calories, 12 g Fat, 8 g Carbohydrate.

ROASTED CAULIFLOWER

2 T. olive oil
2 T. balsamic vinegar
1/2 t. salt

3 cloves garlic, chopped
1 head cauliflower, chopped into
  bite-size pieces

Preheat oven to 450° degrees F. Line a baking sheet with foil. Add the first 4 ingredients. Mix well. Toss with the cauliflower. Spread the mixture on the baking sheet. Bake 20 minutes, stirring occasionally.

Nutritional Information: 86 Calories, 5.7 g Fat, 7.7 g Carbohydrate, 0 mg Cholesterol, 257 mg Sodium, 3.3 g Fiber.

BAKED WHOLE CAULIFLOWER

1 large head cauliflower
1/2 C. seasoned bread crumbs
2 T. grated Parmesan cheese
1/4 C. margarine, melted

1/8 t. garlic powder
1/8 t. salt
1 pinch red pepper flakes
1 pinch dried oregano

Preheat oven to 375 degrees F. Clean and trim the cauliflower. Place in a steamer basket, place in a large pot and add 1 inch of water. Cover, bring to a boil over medium heat. Cook for about 20 minutes. In a bowl, mix the rest of the ingredients. Place the cauliflower in a baking dish. Pour the mixture over the head. Bake for 10 to 15 minutes. Serves 6.

Nutritional Information: 147 Calories, 8.6 g Fat, 14.7 g Carbohydrate, 1 mg Cholesterol, 474 mg Sodium, 5 g Protein, 4 g Fiber.

ROASTED GARLIC CAULIFLOWER

2 T. minced garlic
3 T. olive oil
1 head cauliflower, separated into
 florets

1/3 C. grated Parmesan cheese
Salt and pepper, to taste
1 T. chopped fresh parsley

Preheat oven to 450 degrees F. Spray a casserole dish with non-stick spray. Place the olive oil and garlic in a large resealable bag. Add the cauliflower and shake to mix. Pour into the casserole dish. Bake for 25 minutes, stirring halfway through. Top with the cheese and parsley and broil for 3 to 5 minutes. Serves 6.

Nutritional Information: 123 Calories, 8.5 g Fat, 8.6 g Carbohydrate, 5 mg Cholesterol, 128 mg Sodium, 5.1 g Protein, 3.6 g Fiber.

CHEESY CAULIFLOWER

4 C. small cauliflower florets
1-10 3/4 oz. can 99% fat-free
  condensed cream of mushroom
  soup with 2/3 less salt
1/4 C. evaporated skim milk

1/2 C. finely-grated fat-free
  Cheddar cheese
1/2 C. finely-shredded reduced-fat
  sharp Cheddar cheese

In a large saucepan with a tight-fitting lid, add 1 inch of water and bring to a boil. Place the cauliflower in a steamer basket and set the basket in the pan, making sure the basket sets above the water. Cover and steam for 6 to 8 minutes. In a medium saucepan, stir together the soup and milk. Cook and stir until bubbly. Add the fat-free cheese, cook and stir until melted. Then stir in the reduced-fat cheese. Add the cauliflower. Gently toss until coated and heated through. Makes 4 servings.

Nutritional Information: 117 Calories, 3 g Fat, 11 mg Cholesterol.

GRILLED SALSA ZUCCHINI

1 medium zucchini, sliced
3 tomatoes, diced
1 onion, diced
3 green onions, sliced

2 jalapeño peppers, seeded and
  minced
2 garlic cloves, minced
1 T. minced fresh cilantro
Salt and pepper, to taste

Place the zucchini in foil. In a bowl, add the rest of the ingredients. Pour over the zucchini and seal tightly. Grill over indirect heat for 15 to 20 minutes. Serves 10.

Nutritional Information: 26 Calories, 0 g Fat, 6 g Carbohydrate, 0 mg Cholesterol, 7 mg Sodium, 1 g Protein, 2 g Fiber.

SQUASH AND ZUCCHINI DELIGHT

1 zucchini, sliced
1 squash, sliced
1/2 small cabbage, sliced

1 large onion, sliced
1-14.5 oz. can fat-free chicken
  broth

In a large pot put the first 4 ingredients in. Pour the broth over and bring to a boil over medium heat. Reduce heat to low, cover and simmer for 20 to 30 minutes.

Nutritional Information: 64 Calories, 0.6 g Fat, 11.4 g Carbohydrate, 0 mg Cholesterol, 81 mg Sodium, 4.6 g Protein, 3.7 g Fiber.

ZUCCHINI CAKES

2 C. shredded zucchini
1 C. Italian seasoned bread
  crumbs
1 egg

1 T. mayonnaise
1 t. prepared mustard
1 T. Old Bay seasoning

Preheat oven to 350 degrees F. Spray a baking sheet with non-stick spray. In a large bowl, add all the ingredients. Mix well and form into 7 patties. Place on the baking sheet. Bake for 20 minutes and turn patties. Bake for another 20 minutes. Makes 7 servings.

Nutritional Information: 96 Calories, 3.3 g Fat, 13 g Carbohydrate, 31 mg Cholesterol, 710 mg Sodium, 3.7 g Protein, 1.4 g Fiber.

MAPLE BUTTERNUT SQUASH

1 butternut squash, halved
  lengthwise and seeded
1/4 C. water
1/4 C. maple syrup

1 T. butter, melted
1 T. lemon juice
1/2 t. grated lemon peel

Preheat oven to 350° degrees F. Place squash cut side down in an ungreased 13x9x2-inch baking dish. Add the water. Cover and bake for 50 to 60 minutes. Scoop out the squash and place in a mixing bowl. Add the rest of ingredients and beat until smooth. Serves 4.

Nutritional Information: 186 Calories, 3 g Fat, 42 g Carbohydrate, 8 mg Cholesterol, 41 mg Sodium, 2 g Protein, 8 g Fiber.

ZESTY ZUCCHINI AND SQUASH

3 yellow squash, cubed
3 zucchini, cubed
1-10 oz. can diced tomatoes, with
  green chili peppers

1/2 onion, chopped
Salt, to taste
Garlic powder, to taste

In a large saucepan, combine all the ingredients. Bring to a boil over medium-high heat. Reduce heat to low and cook until tender-crisp. Serves 6.

Nutritional Information: 43 Calories, 0.4 g Fat, 9.7 g Carbohydrate, 0 mg Cholesterol, 328 mg Sodium, 1.8 g Protein, 3 g Fiber.

GLAZED CARROTS AND GINGER

20 baby carrots, peeled but with 1-inch green top left on
1 T. butter
1 T. honey

1-3-inch x 1/2-inch piece ginger, peeled and cut into 1/2-inch-thick matchsticks
1/2 t. thinly-sliced red chili pepper

Bring a pot of water to a boil. Add the carrots and cook until just tender 3 to 4 minutes. Drain carrots and pat dry with paper towels. Melt the butter in a large skillet set over medium-low heat. Add the carrots, honey and ginger. Cook, turning carrots frequently until carrots and ginger are browned, about 8 minutes. Add the pepper and continue to cook until chili is softened, about 1 more minute. Remove from heat and serve. Serves 4.

Nutritional Information: 71 Calories, 3 g Fat, 11 g Carbohydrate, 8 mg Cholesterol, 20 mg Sodium, 1 g Protein, 2 g Fiber.

CRANBERRY-GLAZED CARROTS

8 C. thinly-sliced carrots
4 T. bottled cranberry vinaigrette dressing

1/2 C. canned whole cranberry sauce
1/4 C. chopped toasted pecans

Add the first 3 ingredients to a medium-large non-stick saucepan and bring to a boil. Reduce heat to medium-low and cover the pan. Simmer 8 to 10 minutes, stirring occasionally. Spoon into a serving bowl and sprinkle the pecans over the top. Serves 10.

Nutritional Information: 89 Calories, 3.7 g Fat, 16.5 g Carbohydrate, 0 mg Cholesterol, 60 mg Sodium, 1.5 g Protein, 3.5 g Fiber.

PAN-FRIED CABBAGE

3 slices turkey bacon, cooked and
  crumbled
1/4 c. chopped onion
1/2 head cabbage, cut into
  4 wedges

1 C. low-sodium chicken broth
1/2 t. Splenda
Pepper, to taste
1 1/2 t. cider vinegar

Add the onions to the pan with the turkey bacon drippings and cook over medium heat until light browned. Add the cabbage, broth and sugar to the pan with the onions. Cover pan and cook for 5 minutes, stirring occasionally. Remove cover and cook until the cabbage wilts and broth is almost gone, stirring occasionally. Stir in the turkey bacon pieces and vinegar. Serves 3.

Nutritional Information: 78 Calories, 3.4 g Fat, 7.5 g Carbohydrate, 12 mg Cholesterol, 225 mg Sodium, 5 g Protein, 2.2 g Fiber.

Can I pay for my Visa with Mastercard?

GERMAN RED CABBAGE

2 T. vegetable oil
1/2 C. chopped onion
4 C. shredded red cabbage
1-15 oz. can sliced beets, rinsed,
   drained, cut into sticks
2 T. red wine vinegar

1 T. brown sugar
2 bay leaves
1/8 t. salt
Pinch of ground cloves
Ground black pepper
8 t. low-fat sour cream

Place the oil and onion in a large pot set over medium-low heat. Cook for 3 minutes, or until the onion sizzles. Do not brown. Add the rest of the ingredients, except for the pepper and sour cream. Cook, stirring, for 2 minutes, or until sizzling. Reduce the heat to medium-low. Cover and cook, stirring occasionally, for 30 minutes. Remove and discard the bay leaves. Season with pepper. Serve with a teaspoon dollop of sour cream.

Nutritional Information: 56.3 Calories, 2.3 g Fat, 8.8 g Carbohydrate, 2.1 mg Cholesterol, 150 mg Sodium, 1.2 g Protein, 1.7 g Fiber, 6.1 g Total Sugars.

Ever feel like a Raggedy Ann in a Barbie doll world?

CABBAGE ROLL CASSEROLE

1/2 onion, chopped
1 clove garlic, minced
1/2 small head cabbage, chopped
2 carrots, thinly sliced
1 green bell pepper, chopped
1 C. white rice

2-28 oz. cans diced tomatoes
2 T. packed brown sugar
1/4 C. white vinegar
1 t. dried thyme
1/4 t. salt
1 t. Dijon mustard

Preheat oven to 350 degrees F. Coat a 9x13-inch baking dish with cooking spray. In a bowl, add the first 5 ingredients. Add the rice and mix well. In another large bowl, combine the rest of the ingredients. Stir into the cabbage mixture until blended. Turn into the baking dish. Bake, covered, stirring well every 30 minutes, for 1 1/2 hours. Serves 8.

Nutritional Information: 162.6 Calories, 0.3 g Fat, 37.3 g Carbohydrate, 0 mg Cholesterol, 362.3 mg Sodium, 4.2 g Protein, 5.5 g Fiber, 12.6 Total Sugars.

Can it be a mistake that "stressed" is "desserts" backwards?

GRILLED EGGPLANT

4 eggplants, with the peel, cut
   lengthwise into 1-inch thick
   slices

2 t. kosher salt, divided
4 t. extra-virgin olive oil
1/2 t. black pepper

Layer several paper towels on a baking sheet. Place half of the eggplant in a single layer. Sprinkle with 1 teaspoon of the salt and cover with paper towels. Arrange second layer of eggplant, sprinkle with remaining salt and cover with paper towels. Let eggplant stand 30 minutes, then rinse each piece and blot dry. Brush both sides of an eggplant slice with oil to coat and transfer to a large bowl. Repeat with remaining oil and eggplant slices. Season with the pepper. Heat grill to medium. Grill the eggplant, with cover closed, 16 to 20 minutes, turning once.

Nutritional Information: 117.8 Calories, 7.4 g Fat, 13 g Carbohydrate, 0 mg Cholesterol, 484.6 g Sodium, 2.3 g Protein, 7.7 g Fiber, 5.3 g Total Sugars.

Give up drinking, smoking and fat, and
you'll be really healthy until you kill yourself.

RICE WITH TOMATOES

1 tomato, coarsely chopped
2 t. canola oil
1/4 C. chopped onions
1 clove garlic, minced
1 t. coriander seeds

2/3 C. long-grain aromatic white
rice
1/2 t. powdered ginger
Red pepper flakes

In a blender, purée the tomatoes. Pour into a 2-cup glass measuring cup. Add enough water to bring the level to 1 1/2 cups. Set aside. In a saucepan over medium heat, warm the oil. Add the garlic and coriander seeds and sauté for 2 to 3 minutes. Add the tomatoes, water, ginger and red pepper and bring to a boil. Reduce the heat to low, cover and simmer for 25 to 30 minutes. Remove from the heat and let stand, covered, for 10 minutes.

Nutritional Information: 128.2 Calories, 2.6 g Fat, 24.2 g Carbohydrate, 0 mg Cholesterol, 4.2 mg Sodium, 2.5 g Protein, 1.7 g Fiber, 2.9 g Total Sugars.

MUSHROOM RICE

3/4 C. long-grain rice
1-10 3/4 oz. can reduced-fat beef
broth
3 T. butter

1-8 oz. can sliced mushrooms,
drained
1/2 onion, finely chopped

Preheat oven to 400 degrees F. In a 2-quart baking dish, mix all the ingredients. Bake for 55 minutes.

Nutritional Information: 224.3 Calories, 8.9 g Fat, 31.4 g Carbohydrate, 22.6 mg Cholesterol, 4.7 g Protein, 2 g Fiber, 1.5 g Total Sugar.

SWEET SPICY RICE

1 C. brown rice
1 C. water
1 C. nonfat milk

1 T. cinnamon
1 T. lemon zest
1 t. Splenda

Boil all together for 30 to 35 minutes. Serves 2.

Nutritional Information: 164.6 Calories, 1 g Fat, 29.4 g Carbohydrate, 6.4 g Protein.

ORIENTAL RICE

1 1/2 C. water
1 C. low-fat chicken broth
1 1/3 C. uncooked long-grain
   white rice
2 t. olive oil
2 T. finely-chopped onion
2 T. finely- chopped green pepper

1/2 C. chopped pecans
1/4 t. ground sage
1 C. finely-chopped celery
1-5 oz. can sliced water chestnuts
1/4 t. nutmeg
Black pepper, to taste

Bring the water and broth to a boil. Add rice and stir. Cover and simmer 20 minutes. Remove from heat and let stand, covered, for 5 minutes. Heat oil in large non-stick skillet. Sauté the onion and celery over medium-high heat for 3 minutes. Stir in the remaining ingredients and add the rice. Serves 10.

Nutritional Information: 120.4 Calories, 5.5 g Fat, 16.7 g Carbohydrate, 2 g Protein.

BAKED BROWN RICE

1 1/2 C. brown rice
2 1/3 C. water

2 t. olive oil
1 t. salt

Preheat oven to 375 degrees F. Spread the rice into a 8-inch square glass baking dish. In a covered saucepan on the stove, bring the water and oil to a boil over high heat. Stir in the salt and pour over the rice. Cover and bake 1 hour. Remove from the oven and uncover. Fluff the rice with a fork. Cover with a kitchen towel and let stand 5 minutes. Uncover for another 5 minutes.

Nutritional Information: 117.2 Calories, 1.7 g Fat, 22.9 g Carbohydrate, 2.3 g Protein.

I need a young guy with old cash.

CHINESE FRIED RICE

2 egg whites
1 egg
3/4 t. grated ginger root
1/4 C. chopped fresh mushrooms
1/4 C. finely-shredded carrots
2 T. chopped fresh chives

1 1/2 C. cooked medium-grain
   brown rice, well chilled
3/4 C. chopped Chinese cabbage
1 T. reduced-sodium soy sauce
1/2 t. dry mustard

In a small bowl, beat together the egg whites and egg until well mixed. Lightly spray a large skillet with non-stick spray. Heat the skillet over medium heat. Pour in the eggs. Cook, without stirring, until the eggs begin to set. Then cook and stir until the eggs are crumbly and broken into small bits. Transfer the eggs to a bowl and set aside. Slightly cool the skillet, then spray it again. Heat over the medium-high heat. Add the ginger and cook and stir for 30 seconds. Add the mushrooms, carrots and chives. Cook and stir about 3 minutes, or until the vegetables are tender. Stir in the rice, cabbage and eggs. Sprinkle with the soy sauce and mustard. Cook for 3 to 5 minutes, or until heated, gently tossing to coat the rice with the soy sauce. Makes 6 servings.

Nutritional Information: 80 Calories, 1 g Fat, 36 mg Cholesterol.

Let me call you "Sweethart," I can't remember your name!

HERBED RICE

1 t. olive oil
1 onion, finely chopped
1 garlic clove, minced
1 C. long-grain white rice
1 t. dried Italian seasoning

1/4 t. pepper
1 bay leaf
2 C. vegetable broth
1 t. butter

Heat the oil in a saucepan over medium heat. Add the onion and garlic. Cook 5 minutes. Add the rice. Cook 1 minute. Add the seasonings, bay leaf and broth. Heat to boiling. Reduce the heat to low, cover and simmer 20 minutes. Remove from the heat and discard the bay leaf. Stir in butter. Makes 4 servings.

Nutritional Information: 141 Calories, 3 g Fat, 26 g Carbohydrate, 3 mg Cholesterol, 514 mg Sodium, 3 g Protein, 1 g Fiber.

GRILLED ASPARAGUS

1 lb. asparagus
1 T. olive oil

1 clove garlic, minced
1 oz. Parmesan cheese

Mix the olive oil, garlic and cheese. Pour over the asparagus and coat well. Place on the grill and grill about 20 minutes. Serves 4.

Nutritional Information: 81 Calories, 5.7 g Fat, 4 g Carbohydrate, 4.7 g Protein.

ROASTED ASPARAGUS SPEARS

3/4 lb. asparagus spears
1 1/2 t. olive oil
1/2 t. minced garlic

1 t. balsamic vinegar
2 T. grated Parmesan cheese
Salt and pepper, to taste

Preheat oven to 450 degrees F. Trim the ends of the asparagus. Spray a small baking sheet with cooking spray. Mix the oil and garlic. Arrange the asparagus in a single layer. Drizzle with olive oil and garlic mixture. Roast for 12 to 15 minutes. Place on a serving dish and sprinkle with the rest of the ingredients. Serves 2.

Nutritional Information: 94.1 Calories, 5.2 g Fat, 8.5 g Carbohydrate, 6 g Protein.

ASPARAGUS ROLLS

3 asparagus spears
2 T. low-fat shredded Cheddar
  cheese
2 T. shredded Monterey Jack
  cheese

Dash of Tabasco sauce
1/4 C. 2% milk
1 slice bread
Melted butter

Preheat oven to 350° degrees F. Remove the crust on the bread. Roll out the bread with a rolling pin and flatten. Melt the cheese in a saucepan with the milk. Add the Tabasco. Spread on the bread and top with the asparagus spears. Roll up and cut in half. Brush with the melted butter. Bake for 15 to 20 minutes. Serves 1.

Nutritional Information: 190 Calories, 7 g Fat, 19 g Carbohydrate, 20 mg Cholesterol, 380 mg Sodium, 12 g Protein, 2 g Fiber.

DILL MUSTARD ASPARAGUS

2 C. water
1 lb. asparagus spears, trimmed
1 T. light tub margarine
2 t. Dijon mustard

1 T. snipped fresh dill weed, or 1 t.
   dried
1/8 t. salt

In a large non-stick skillet, bring the water to a boil over high heat. Add the asparagus. Reduce the heat, simmer, covered, for 2 minutes. In a small bowl, add the rest of the ingredients. Drain the asparagus and place on a serving dish. Spoon the mixture on top and toss until covered. Serves 6.

Nutritional Information: 29 Calories, 1 g Fat, 3 g Carbohydrate, 0 mg Cholesterol, 106 mg Sodium, 2 g Protein, 2 g Fiber.

BREADED BRUSSELS SPROUTS

Jane Brandon, St. Lake City, VT

1 1/2 lb. Brussels sprouts
1 t. salt
4 T. butter, melted
4 T. grated Parmesan cheese

4 T. dried bread crumbs
1/4 t. garlic powder
1/4 t. black pepper
1/4 t. seasoning salt

Wash and trim the Brussels sprouts. Cut an X about 1/8-inch deep in the stem of the sprouts. In a medium-size pot, cover the sprouts with water and add the salt. Bring to a boil. Cover and simmer for 6 minutes or until tender. Drain. Place the sprouts in a casserole dish. Sprinkle 2 tablespoons of the melted butter and mix well. Combine the rest of the ingredients and sprinkle the mixture over the sprouts. Place sprouts on a baking sheet. Broil for about 5 minutes. Serves 12.

Nutritional Information: 75 Calories, 4.6 g Fat, 6.9 g Carbohydrate, 12 mg Cholesterol, 316 mg Sodium, 2.9 g Protein, 2.2 g Fiber.

BRUSSELS SPROUTS IN MUSTARD SAUCE

2 T. cornstarch
1/4 C. water
1-14.5 oz. can low-fat chicken
  broth

1 lb. Brussels sprouts
2 t. prepared Dijon mustard
1 t. lemon juice

Dissolve cornstarch in 1/4 cup water and set aside. In a saucepan over medium heat, bring the chicken broth to a boil. Add the sprouts and cook until tender. Strain, reserving the chicken broth and place in a warm serving dish. Return chicken broth to the stove and stir in the mustard and lemon juice. Return to a boil. Add the cornstarch mixture. Cook and stir until thickened. Pour over the sprouts to serve. Serves 6.

Nutritional Information: 46 Calories, 0.6 g Fat, 9.7 g Carbohydrate, 2 mg Cholesterol, 391 mg Sodium, 2.3 g Protein, 2 g Fiber.

SCALLOPED BRUSSELS SPROUTS

1 lb. fresh Brussels sprouts,
  steamed and drained
1 C. nonfat sour cream
2 T. fresh lemon juice

3 T. shredded Parmesan cheese,
  divided
2 t. sesame seeds

Preheat the broiler. In a bowl, add the sour cream, lemon juice and 1 1/2 tablespoons Parmesan cheese. Stir in the Brussels sprouts. Pour into a baking dish and sprinkle with the remaining Parmesan cheese and sesame seeds. Broil for 3 to 5 minutes. Serves 6.

Nutritional Information: 89 Calories, 1.5 g Fat, 13 g Carbohydrate, 9 mg Cholesterol, 104 mg Sodium, 5 g Protein, 3 g Fiber.

GREEN BEAN CASSEROLE

1 T. butter, melted
1 C. fat-free sour cream
2 T. flour
1 t. salt
1 t. sugar
1/2 C. chopped onion

1-16 oz. bag frozen French-style
  green beans
1 C. shredded, reduced-fat
  Cheddar cheese
1/2 C. crumbled reduced-fat Ritz
  crackers
Canola cooking spray

Preheat oven to 350 degrees F. Coat a 9x9-inch baking dish with canola cooking spray. Stir the butter and 2 tablespoons of the sour cream. Add the flour. Add the remaining sour cream, salt and sugar. Stir until well blended. In a large bowl, blend the sour cream mixture with the green beans and half of the Cheddar cheese. Spread mixture into the prepared baking dish. Spread the remaining cheese over the top and top with cracker crumbs. Spray the cracker topping lightly with the canola cooking spray. Bake 30 to 35 minutes. Serves 9.

Nutritional Information: 115 Calories, 4 g Fat, 4 g Carbohydrate, 10 mg Cholesterol, 368 mg Sodium, 6 g Protein, 1.5 g Fiber.

I drive way too fast to worry about cholesterol.

GRILLED GREEN BEANS WITH GORGONZOLA VINAIGRETTE

6 C. lightly-salted boiling water
1 lb. fresh green beans, ends
    trimmed
1 T. olive oil, divided
1/4 C. balsamic vinegar
1/4 C. crumbled Gorgonzola
    cheese

1 T. firmly-packed brown sugar
4 cloves garlic, minced
1 green onion, chopped
1/2 t. chopped fresh thyme
1/2 t. chopped fresh basil
Salt and pepper, to taste

Add the beans to the boiling water and cook for 4 to 5 minutes. Remove from the heat. Drain and immerse in ice water. Drain and set aside. In a small saucepan over medium heat, add 1 1/2 teaspoons of the olive oil, vinegar, Gorgonzola cheese, brown sugar, garlic, green onion, thyme and basil. Cook just until the ingredients start to combine, approximately 7 minutes. Remove from the heat. Toss the green beans in the remaining olive oil and salt and pepper. Grill the beans for 1 to 2 minutes. Remove and toss with the vinaigrette. Serves 6.

Nutritional Information: 73.5 Calories, 5.5 g Fat.

I'd do anything to be thin, except diet and exercise.

MEDITERRANEAN GREEN BEANS

8 garlic cloves, unpeeled
1 T. pine nuts
1/2 C. boiling water
4 dry-packed sun-dried tomato
  halves
1 t. olive oil

1-9 oz. pkg. frozen no-salt-added
  cut green beans, thawed
1 T. snipped fresh dill weed, or 1 t.
  dried
1/2 t. pepper
2 T. shredded Parmesan cheese

Preheat the oven to 350° degrees F. Place the garlic cloves on an ungreased non-stick baking sheet. Roast for 15 minutes. Add the pine nuts and roast for 5 more minutes. Remove and cool. In a small bowl, combine the water and tomatoes. Let stand for 10 to 15 minutes. Drain well, discarding the water. Cut the tomatoes into thin slices. Squeeze the garlic out of the skins into a small bowl. Heat a large non-stick skillet over medium heat. Pour the oil into the skillet and swirl to coat the bottom. Cook the garlic for 15 seconds, stirring constantly. Stir in the green beans, cooking for 3 to 5 minutes. Stir in the tomatoes, dill weed and pepper. Cook for 1 minute, stirring. Sprinkle with the Parmesan cheese and pine nuts. Serves 4.

Nutritional Information: 72 Calories, 3 g Fat, 9 g Carbohydrate, 2 mg Cholesterol, 46 mg Sodium, 3 g Protein, 2 g Fiber.

I know I'm in my own little world, but it's ok, they know me here.

SPICY CREAM CORN

1 t. olive oil
1 yellow onion, finely chopped
1/2 red bell pepper, diced
1 jalapeño, seeded and finely
  chopped
2 cloves garlic, finely chopped

1-12 oz. box frozen corn
2 t. flour
3/4 C. 1% milk
1/4 C. reduced-fat chicken broth
Fresh cilantro, chopped

Heat the oil in a skillet over medium heat. Add the onion, red bell pepper and jalapeño, stirring occasionally. When softened slightly, add the garlic and corn. Once the corn is warm, sprinkle with the flour. Stir and let cook for 1 minute. Add the milk and broth. Let the mixture simmer and reduce for about 5 minutes, stirring occasionally. Remove from the heat and stir in cilantro. Serves 4.

Nutritional Information: 139.7 Calories, 2.5 g Fat, 28.3 g Carbohydrate, 5.3 g Protein.

SWEET CORN CASSEROLE

2 C. fresh sweet corn, cutting the
  kernels from the cob
1-14.5 oz. can low-sodium cream-
  style corn

1-8.5 oz. box corn muffin mix
1 C. low-fat buttermilk
2 T. melted light stick butter

Preheat the oven to 400 degrees F. Spray a 9x13-inch glass baking dish. Place the kernels in a mixing bowl and add the rest of the ingredients and stir until completely mixed. Pour into the dish. Bake 40 to 50 minutes. Serves 12.

Nutritional Information: 149.2 Calories, 1.6 g Fat, 13.7 g Carbohydrate, 2.2 g Protein.

MEXICAN-STYLE CORN

4 large ears sweet corn, cutting the kernels from the cobs
1 C. cherry tomatoes, halved
3 jalapeño peppers, seeded and chopped

1 onion, chopped
2 T. canola oil
1 t. salt
1/2 t. black pepper

Heat the canola oil in a skillet. Sauté the onion until it is lightly browned. Add the peppers and sauté another minute. Add the corn and tomatoes and heat through. Season with salt and pepper. Serves 4.

Nutritional Information: 209.7 Calories, 8.9 g Fat, 32.9 g Carbohydrate, 0 mg Cholesterol, 601.8 mg Sodium, 5.5 g Protein, 5.3 g Fiber.

CORN PUDDING

Vegetable oil spray
2 C. frozen no-salt-added whole kernel corn, thawed
1 1/4 C. fat-free buttermilk
2 eggs

1 T. light tub margarine, melted
1 t. sugar
1/4 t. salt
1/4 t. white pepper

Preheat the oven to 350 degrees F. Lightly spray a 6 1/2-inch square baking dish with the vegetable oil. Combine all the ingredients in a bowl. Pour into the baking dish. Bake for 45 to 50 minutes. Remove from the oven and let set 5 minutes. Serves 4.

Nutritional Information: 133 Calories, 2.5 g Fat, 22 g Carbohydrate, 3 mg Cholesterol, 313 mg Sodium, 8 g Protein, 2 g Fiber.

SPICY BLACK BEANS

1 can black beans, with liquid
1 onion, chopped
1 clove garlic, chopped

1 T. fresh cilantro, chopped
1/4 t. cayenne pepper
Salt, to taste

Combine the beans, onion and garlic in a pot and bring to a boil. Reduce to medium-low heat. Season with the rest of the ingredients and simmer 5 minutes. Serves 4.

Nutritional Information: 121.6 Calories, 0.5 g Fat, 22.2 g Carbohydrate, 7.9 g Protein.

BAKED BEANS

2 C. black-eyed peas, dry
1 onion, chopped
1 ham hock
4 slices peppered bacon
2/3 C. sugar-free syrup

2 t. salt
1 t. pepper
1 t. ground mustard
4 C. water

Place the beans in a bowl, covered, with 2 inches of water for at least 8 hours. Preheat oven to 300 degrees F. Drain the peas and put in a large pot on the stove. Add the rest of the ingredients and bring to a boil. Tightly put the lid on the pot and transfer to the oven. Cook for 2 hours, then remove the lid and cook for another 1 to 1 1/2 hours. Serves 8.

Nutritional Information: 127.9 Calories, 2.6 g Fat, 22.1 g Carbohydrate, 6 g Protein.

SPANISH BLACK BEANS

2 T. olive oil
2 onions, chopped
6 cloves garlic, chopped
1-19 oz. can black beans, rinsed
   and drained
1-16 oz. can tomato sauce

2 tomatoes, diced
2 t. ground cumin
1/2 t. cayenne pepper
3/4 C. chopped fresh cilantro
1/2 C. chopped green onions
1/4 C. chopped fresh cilantro

Heat the olive oil in a large pot over medium-high heat. Cook the onions and garlic until the onions are translucent, about 5 to 7 minutes. Stir in the black beans, tomato sauce, diced tomatoes, cumin and cayenne pepper. Reduce the heat to medium-low and simmer 5 minutes. Add the 3/4 cup cilantro and simmer another 2 minutes. Stir in the green onions and remove from the heat. Garnish with the 1/4 cup of cilantro. Serves 6.

Nutritional Information: 179 Calories, 5.3 g Fat, 27.5 g Carbohydrate, 0 mg Cholesterol, 753 mg Sodium, 8 g Protein, 9.2 g Fiber.

NAVY BEANS AND TOMATOES

1 lb. bag dry navy beans
8 C. water
1 onion, chopped
6 cloves garlic, chopped
1 stalk celery, chopped
15 baby carrots, sliced

4 chicken bouillon cubes
1/4 t. pepper
2 T. dried parsley
1-14.5 oz. can tomato sauce
1-14.5 oz. can diced tomatoes

Place the first 9 ingredients into a pot. Bring to a boil and reduce heat and simmer for at least 2 hours. Add the tomato sauce and diced tomatoes. Simmer for 15 to 20 minutes. Serves 8.

Nutritional Information: 195.8 Calories, 0.3 g Fat, 44.9 g Carbohydrate, 14.8 g Protein.

DESSERTS

NOTES

_____

_____

_____

_____

_____

_____

_____

_____

_____

_____

_____

_____

_____

_____

_____

_____

_____

CHOCOLATE LAYER CAKE

1 C. + 2 T. flour
1/3 C. unsweetened cocoa powder
1 t. instant-coffee granules
1 t. baking powder
1 t. baking soda
1/4 t. salt
1/4 C. + 2 T. sugar

2 T. unsalted butter, softened
1 large egg
1 t. vanilla extract
1 C. fat-free buttermilk
1/2 C. raspberry spreadable fruit
1 T. confectioners' sugar

Preheat the oven to 350 degrees F. Spray 2-8-inch square baking pans with non-stick spray. In a bowl, combine the flour, cocoa powder, instant coffee, baking powder, baking soda and salt. In another bowl, with an electric mixer on high speed, cream the sugar and butter. Add the egg and vanilla, beating until smooth. Gradually beat in the flour mixture alternately with the buttermilk, until the batter is smooth. Pour the batter into the pans. Bake for 15 to 20 minutes. Remove the cakes from the pan. In a saucepan, melt the spreadable fruit, 2 to 3 minutes. Brush on the top of bottom layer. Add the top layer and spread the fruit on top. Sprinkle with confectioners' sugar. Serves 12.

Nutritional Information: 135 Calories, 3 g Fat, 25 g Carbohydrate, 24 mg Cholesterol, 215 mg Sodium, 1 g Fiber.

Lord, keep your arm around my shoulder and your hand on my mouth.

COCOA FUDGE CAKE

1 1/2 C. flour
1/2 C. unsweetened cocoa powder
1 t. baking powder
1 t. baking soda
2 T. margarine

2/3 C. sugar
2 eggs
1 t. vanilla extract
1 1/2 C. buttermilk
1/2 c. nonfat sour cream

Preheat oven to 350 degrees F. Spray an 8-inch round baking pan with non-stick cooking spray and dust it lightly with flour. Set aside. In a small bowl, stir together the flour, cocoa powder, baking powder and baking soda. In another bowl, cream together the margarine and sugar. Beat in the eggs, one at a time. Add the vanilla and half the buttermilk, then stir in half the dry ingredients. Add the remaining buttermilk and beat well. Add the remaining dry ingredients. Pour the batter in the pan. Bake 35 to 40 minutes. Let the cake cool 5 minutes. Top each portion with some sour cream. Makes 10 servings.

Nutritional Information: 180 Calories, 4 g Fat, 44 mg Cholesterol, 177 mg Sodium, 0 g Fiber.

*If you can't be a good example, you'll
just have to serve as a horrible warning.*

PUMPKIN CAKE WITH CHEESE GLAZE

1 1/2 C. sugar
1/2 C. butter, softened
3/4 C. egg substitute
1 t. vanilla extract
1-15 oz. can pumpkin
3 C. cake flour

1 t. baking powder
1 t. baking soda
1 t. ground cinnamon
1/2 t. salt
1/4 t. ground ginger
1/4 t. ground nutmeg

Glaze:
1/2 C. powdered sugar
1/2 C. 1/3-less-fat cream cheese,
  softened

1/2 t. vanilla extract
3 T. fresh orange juice

Preheat oven to 350 degrees F. Coat a 10-inch tube pan with cooking spray. Mix sugar and butter in a bowl. Beat with a mixer until well blended, about 5 minutes. Add the egg substitute, 1/4 cup at a time, beating well after each addition. Beat in the vanilla and pumpkin. Combine the flour and next 6 ingredients, stirring well with a whisk. Fold in the flour mixture with the pumpkin mixture. Spoon batter into the pan. Bake for 55 minutes. Cool in the pan 10 minutes on a wire rack. Turn out on the wire rack. Place the powdered sugar and cream cheese in a bowl and beat with a mixer at medium speed until well blended. Beat in the vanilla and orange juice. Drizzle glaze over the warm cake. Cool completely on the wire rack. Serves 16.

Nutritional Information: 236 Calories, 7.5 g Fat, 38.8 g Carbohydrate, 21 mg Cholesterol, 295 mg Sodium, 3.9 g Protein, 1.5 g Fiber.

RUM CAKE

Sally Moore, Jonestown, PA

1/4 C. instant nonfat dry milk
1/4 C. sugar
1 C. hot water
1 pkg. quick-rising active dry
  yeast
2 3/4 C. flour

1 t. salt
1 t. vanilla extract
1/4 C. margarine, softened
1/2 C. egg whites, at room
  temperature

Rum Sauce:
1 C. sugar
1/2 C. light corn syrup

1/2 C. water
1/4 C. rum

Preheat the oven when ready to use to 350 degrees F. In a bowl, add the dry milk and sugar. Add the hot water and mix to dissolve the sugar. Cool. Add the yeast and mix lightly. Let stand about 10 minutes. Add 1 1/2 cups of the flour and mix at medium speed, using a dough hook for 4 minutes. Add the salt, vanilla, margarine, egg whites and remaining flour and mix again for 4 minutes. Spread the batter evenly in a greased 10-inch tube pan. Cover with a cloth and let rise at room temperature until doubled in volume. Bake for 50 to 60 minutes. While the cake is baking, prepare the rum sauce. Combine the first 3 ingredients in a saucepan. Stir over low heat until the sugar is dissolved. Then simmer, uncovered, for 5 minutes. Remove the syrup from the heat and add the rum. Let stand at room temperature until needed. When the cake is done, let it cool in the pan for 5 minutes. Turn out onto a wire rack and puncture about 15 holes in the bottom of the cake with a meat fork. Pour the syrup in the bottom of the cake pan and return the cake to the pan. Let stand at room temperature for about 30 minutes to absorb the syrup. Turn out onto a platter. Serves 20.

Nutritional Information: 231 Calories, 8 g Fat, 36 g Carbohydrate, 1 mg Cholesterol, 383 mg Sodium, 5 g Protein.

CARROT CAKE

2 1/2 C. unbleached flour
1 1/3 C. sugar
2 t. baking soda
2 t. cinnamon
2-8 oz. cans crushed pineapple, with juice

1/4 c. skim milk
4 egg whites, lightly beaten
2 t. vanilla
2 C. grated carrots, packed
1/2 c. raisins

Cream Cheese Frosting:
8 oz. nonfat cream cheese
1/2 C. nonfat ricotta cheese

1/2 C. confectioners' sugar
1 t. vanilla

Preheat the oven to 325 degrees F. Coat a 9x13-inch pan with non-stick cooking spray. Combine the first 4 ingredients and mix well. Stir in the pineapple, milk, egg whites and vanilla. Fold in the carrots and raisins. Pour in the batter and spread evenly in the pan. Bake for 35 minutes. Cool to room temperature. Combine all the ingredients for the frosting and mix well. Spread over the cake.

Nutritional Information: 215 Calories, 0.3 g Fat, 3 mg Cholesterol, 268 mg Sodium, 7.7 g Protein, 1.4 g Fiber.

Dear Santa, I can explain.

ANGEL CAKE SURPRISE

1 angel food cake
1-3 oz. pkg. strawberry flavored
   gelatin
1-15 oz. can sliced peaches
3 bananas, sliced

1-5 oz. pkg. instant vanilla
   pudding mix
1-8 oz. container frozen whipped
   topping, thawed
1-20 oz. can crushed pineapple,
   drained

Break the angel food cake into bite-size pieces. Place in a 9x13-inch glass pan. Dissolve the package of gelatin in 1 cup of water. Pour over the cake pieces, spreading to the edges of the pan. Drain the peaches and pour the juice over the gelatin in the pan. Place the bananas on top of the gelatin. Arrange the peach slices on top of the bananas. Prepare the pudding according to the instructions on the box and spread evenly on the fruit. Spread the whipped topping on top of the pudding. Refrigerate at least 2 hours before serving. Serves 24.

Nutritional Information: 166 Calories, 2.6 g Fat, 34.9 g Carbohydrate, 224 mg Sodium, 2.2 g Protein, 0.7 gm Fiber.

LEMON PUDDING CAKE

2 T. butter, room temperature
1/4 C. sugar
1/4 C. Splenda
1/8 t. salt
6 egg whites, room temperature,
   divided

3 T. flour
1 T. grated lemon zest
1/4 C. fresh lemon juice, strained
1 C. skim milk
Boiled water

Preheat oven to 325 degrees F. Adjust oven rack to center position. Lightly spray with non-stick spray, 6 custard cups. In a blender, add the butter, sugar, Splenda and salt and mix until crumbly. Add 3 egg whites and flour, mixing until smooth. Slowly add the lemon zest and juice. Add the milk and mix. In a large bowl, beat remaining 3 egg whites until stiff peaks form. Gently whisk whites into batter just until blended. Ladle batter into custard cups. Set a large roasting pan onto oven rack. Lay a folded dish towel onto bottom of roasting pan. Set the cups on top of the towel. Pour enough boiling water into the roasting pan to come halfway up the sides of the custard cups. Bake 20 to 25 minutes, or until pudding cake center is set. Remove from oven and set on a wire rack. Let cups continue to stand in water for 10 minutes. Serve at room temperature. Sprinkle with powdered sugar just before serving.

Nutritional Information: 114.8 Calories, 3.7 g Fat.

Stop me before I volunteer again.

GERMAN APPLE CAKE

1 C. raisins
2 3/4 C. flour
1/4 C. water
3/4 C. sugar
3/4 C. brown sugar
1/2 t. cinnamon
1/2 t. nutmeg
1/4 t. ground cloves
1/2 t. allspice
2 t. baking soda

1 t. baking powder
1 1/2 C. nonfat plain yogurt
1 3/4 C. applesauce
1/3 C. canola oil
1 t. vanilla extract
4 egg whites
3 C. apples, chopped
1/4 C. walnuts, chopped
1/4 C. Grape-Nuts cereal

Preheat oven to 350 degrees F. Spray two 9x9-inch pans with cooking spray. Combine raisins and water in a small bowl. Microwave for 1 minute, set aside. In a large bowl, add the flour, sugars, spices, baking powder and baking soda. Add the yogurt, applesauce, oil, vanilla and egg whites to the dry ingredients. Mix well. Add the chopped apples, raisins, walnuts and Grape-Nuts to the batter. Mix well. Pour into the two pans. Bake for 25 to 30 minutes, or until center tests clean. Serves 30.

Nutritional Information: 140 Calories, 3 g Fat, 0 g Saturated Fat, 26 g Carbohydrate, 0 mg Cholesterol, 120 mg Sodium, 3 g Protein, 1 g Fiber, 16 g Sugar.

COCONUT CREAM PIE

1 crust, rolled refrigerated
  unbaked pie crust, cooked
  according to directions
1/4 C. sugar
1/4 C. cornstarch
1 1/2 C. fat-free milk
1-12 oz. can evaporated fat-free
  milk

3 eggs, separated
3 T. flaked coconut
1/2 t. coconut flavoring
3 egg whites
1/2 t. vanilla
1/4 t. cream of tartar
1/3 C. sugar
2 T. flaked coconut

In a saucepan, combine the 1/4 cup sugar and cornstarch. Stir in the two milks. Cook and stir over medium heat until thickened and bubbly. Cook and stir for 2 more minutes. Remove from the heat. Slowly stir about 1 cup of the hot filling into the egg yolks and return the yolks to the saucepan. Bring to a gentle boil and reduce heat to medium low. Cook and stir for 2 minutes more. Remove from the heat. Stir in 3 tablespoons of the coconut and coconut flavoring. Cover and keep warm. In a medium bowl, combine the egg whites, vanilla and cream of tartar. Beat with an electric mixer on medium speed until soft peaks form. Slowly add the 1/3 cup sugar, 1 tablespoon at a time, beating on high speed about 2 minutes, or until stiff peaks form and sugar is dissolved. Pour the pie mixture into the crust, and spread the meringue over the filling. Sprinkle with 2 tablespoons coconut. Bake for 15 minutes. Cool on a wire rack for an hour. Chill for 3 to 6 hours before serving. Serves 10.

Nutritional Information: 191 Calories, 4 g Total Fat, 2 g Saturated Fat, 29 g Carbohydrate, 64 mg Cholesterol, 212 mg Sodium, 6 g Protein, 0 g Fiber.

STRAWBERRY PIE

2 1/2 C. strawberries
1/4 C. sugar
1 envelope unflavored gelatin
2 T. frozen limeade
3 slightly-beaten egg whites
3 T. orange juice, divided

1-3 oz. pkg. ladyfingers, split
1/2-8 oz. container frozen light
  whipped dessert topping,
  thawed
Sliced strawberries

Place the strawberries in a blender. Blend until nearly smooth. You should have about 1 1/2 cups. In a medium saucepan, stir together the sugar and gelatin. Stir in the strawberries and limeade. Cook and stir over medium heat until the mixture bubbles and the gelatin is dissolved. Gradually stir about half of the gelatin mixture into the egg whites. Return mixture to the saucepan. Cook, stirring constantly, over low heat about 3 minutes, or until mixture is slightly thickened. Do not boil. Pour into a medium bowl. Stir in 1 tablespoon of the orange juice. Chill until mixture mounds when spooned, stirring occasionally, about 2 hours. Cut half of the split ladyfingers in half crosswise and stand on end around the outside edge of a 9-inch springform pan. Arrange remaining split ladyfingers in the bottom of the pan. Drizzle the 2 tablespoons orange juice over the ladyfingers. Fold whipped topping into strawberry mixture. Spoon into pan. Cover and chill about 2 hours. Garnish with sliced strawberries. Serves 8.

Nutritional Information: 170 Calories, 3 g Fat, Trace of Saturated Fat, 15.5% Calories from Fat, 32 g Carbohydrate, 39 mg Cholesterol, 74 mg Sodium, 4 g Protein, 1 g Dietary Fiber.

FROZEN MANGO CREAM PIE

10 low-fat graham crackers
2 T. sugar
3 T. light butter, melted
3 large mangos, peeled and
  coarsely chopped
1 1/4 C. sugar, divided into 3/4 C.
  and 1/2 C.
1/4 C. fresh lime juice

1-8 oz. light cream cheese
1-8 oz. fat-free Cool Whip
1 large mango, peeled and thinly
  sliced
2 T. sugar
2 T. fresh lime juice
1 T. orange liquor

Preheat oven to 375 degrees F. Crush the graham crackers to make crumbs, about 1 1/2 cups. Place crumbs, 2 tablespoons sugar and 3 tablespoons melted butter in the bottom of a 9inch springform pan. Pat crust evenly over the bottom of the pan. Bake for 8 minutes, remove from oven and set aside to cool. In a blender, purée the 3 mangos with the 1/2 cup sugar, 1/4 cup lime juice and orange liquor until smooth. Place the cream cheese and 3/4 cup sugar in a large bowl and beat with a mixer at medium speed until smooth. With the mixer on low, pour the mango purée into the cream cheese mixture and beat together until mixed well. Fold the whipped topping gently into the mango/cheese mixture until well blended. Pour mixture into pan, smoothing out the top. Cover with foil and freeze until firm at least 4 hours or overnight. When ready to serve, gently toss the 1 mango with the 2 tablespoons sugar and 2 tablespoons lime juice. Serve on top of each slice. Serves 12.

Nutritional Information: 264 Calories, 6 g Total Fat, 4 g Saturated Fat, 49 g Carbohydrate, 145 mg Sodium, 3 g Protein, 2 g Fiber, 4 Weight Watcher Points.

BANANA PIE

10-inch prepared pie shell
1/3 C. sweetened shredded
  coconut
8 vanilla wafers
2 barely ripe bananas, cut in
  diagonal slices

2/3 C. sugar
1/4 C. cornstarch
2 egg yolks
3 C. vanilla soy milk
2 t. fresh lemon juice
1 t. vanilla extract

Preheat oven to 350 degrees F. Bake pie shell according to package directions. Keep oven on. Spread the coconut on a baking sheet. Bake until toasted, stirring occasionally, about 5 minutes. Transfer to a small bowl. Set aside. Place the vanilla wafers in a zipper-type bag and seal. With a rolling pin, crush to coarse crumbs. Add to the coconut. Mix well. Set aside. In a saucepan, add the sugar and cornstarch. In a large bowl, whisk egg yolks to blend, then whisk in the soy milk. Whisk 1/2 cup milk mixture in the sugar until smooth. Whisk in remaining milk. Bring to a boil and stir constantly with a whisk. Boil 1 minute, then remove from heat. Stir in lemon juice and vanilla. Mix in the bananas. Pour into the pie shell. Let stand 10 minutes to cool. Refrigerate for 6 to 8 hours. Just before serving, sprinkle with the coconut crumb topping. Serves 10.

Nutritional Information: 160 Calories, 5 g Fat, 2 g Saturated Fat, 27 g Carbohydrate, 45 mg Cholesterol, 40 mg Sodium, 3 g Protein, 2 g Fiber, 20 g Sugar.

BLACKBERRY COBBLER

1/4 C. butter
1/2 C. sugar
1 C. flour
1/4 t. salt
2 t. baking powder

1/2 C. skim milk
1 1/2 C. frozen blackberries
1/2 C. sugar
1 C. skim milk

Preheat oven to 375 degrees F. Spray a 10x5x3-quart casserole dish with cooking spray. Cream the butter and 1/2 cup sugar until light and fluffy. Stir together the flour, salt and baking powder. Add flour mixture to the creamed butter mixture alternately with 1/2 cup milk. Beat until smooth. Pour into the prepared pan. Spoon berries over the batter. Sprinkle 1/2 cup sugar over the berries. Pour 1 cup milk over the top. Bake for 45 to 50 minutes. Batter will rise to the top and create a custard within. Serves 8.

Nutritional Information: 184 Calories, 5 g Fat, 34 g Carbohydrate, 13 mg Cholesterol, 211 mg Sodium, 2 g Protein, 2 g Dietary Fiber.

Easy as pie, my ass!

CHERRY AND APPLE COBBLER

3/4 C. flour
1/4 C. whole wheat flour
1/4 C. sugar
1 1/2 t. baking powder
1 t. finely-shredded orange peel
1 t. ground cinnamon
3 T. butter
1/4 C. cold water

4 t. cornstarch
1-16 oz. pkg. frozen unsweetened
   pitted tart red cherries
3 C. thinly-sliced apples
1/3 C. fat-free milk
1/4 C. refrigerated egg substitute
   or 1 egg

Preheat oven to 400 degrees F. In a bowl, combine flours, 2 tablespoons sugar, baking powder, orange peel and 1/2 teaspoon cinnamon. Cut in the butter until mixture resembles coarse crumbs. Set aside. In a saucepan, combine the water, cornstarch, sugar and cinnamon. Add the frozen cherries. Cook until thickened and bubbly, stirring. Stir in the apples and heat. Reduce heat. In a bowl, combine the milk and egg. Add to the flour mixture, stirring until moistened. Place the hot filling in a 2-quart baking dish. Spoon the biscuit topping into nine mounds on top of filling. Bake 18 to 20 minutes. Serve warm. Serves 9.

Nutritional Information: 164 Calories, 4 g Total Fat, 3 g Saturated Fat, 30 g Carbohydrate, 10 mg Cholesterol, 87 mg Sodium, 3 g Protein, 3 g Fiber.

BLUEBERRY COBBLER

2 C. fresh or frozen unsweetened
   blueberries, thawed
3 T. maple syrup
1/2 C. flour
1/4 t. baking powder

1/2 t. ground cinnamon
1/8 t. salt
1 T. + 1 1/2 t. margarine, melted
1 T. skim milk
1 t. grated lemon zest

Preheat the oven to 400 degrees F. Lightly spray a 9-inch pie plate with non-stick cooking spray. Set aside. In a saucepan, combine the blueberries and maple syrup and cook over medium heat, stirring occasionally, 5 minutes. In a bowl, combine the flour, baking powder, cinnamon and salt. Stir. Stir in the margarine, milk and lemon zest and mix until a soft dough forms. Turn the dough onto a lightly floured surface and roll it out with a floured rolling pin. Pour the berry mixture in the pan and place the crust on top. Bake for 25 minutes. Let it cook 5 minutes. Makes 4 servings.

Nutritional Information: 177 Calories, 5 g Fat, 0 mg Cholesterol, 129 mg Sodium, 2 g Fiber.

A man's home is his castle until the queen arrives.

PUMPKIN CHEESECAKE

3/4 C. finely-crushed graham crackers
2 T. margarine, melted
1-15 oz. carton low-fat ricotta cheese
1-8 oz. tub fat-free cream cheese
1 C. canned pumpkin
1/2 C. skim milk

1 envelope unflavored gelatin
2 t. finely-shredded orange peel
1/2 C. orange juice
1/3 C. sugar
1/3 C. packed brown sugar
2 t. vanilla
1 t. pumpkin spice

In a mixing bowl, stir together the crackers and margarine until moistened. Press into the bottom of a 9-inch springform pan. Refrigerate, until ready to fill. In a blender, add half of the ricotta cheese, half of the pumpkin and half of the milk. Blend until smooth. Place in a mixing bowl. Repeat with the same ingredients. In a saucepan, sprinkle the gelatin over the orange juice. Let stand 5 minutes. Cook, stirring, over low heat until gelatin is dissolved. Stir into the pumpkin mixture. Add the rest of the ingredients and mix well. Pour mixture into the crust. Cover and refrigerate for at least 4 hours. Serves 12.

Nutritional Information: 142 Calories, 2 g Total Fat, 0 g Saturated Fat, 23 g Carbohydrate, 7 mg Cholesterol, 214 mg Sodium, 11 g Protein, 1 g Fiber.

CHEESECAKE

1 C. nonfat granola, crushed
2-8 oz. pkg. nonfat cream cheese
4 egg whites
1/4 C. sugar
1 t. lemon juice

Pinch of salt
2 t. vanilla
1/2 pt. nonfat sour cream
2 t. sugar
1 t. vanilla

Preheat oven to 250 degrees F. Press the granola into a sprayed 10-inch pie pan. Beat the cream cheese with a mixer to soften and to get creamy. Add the next 5 ingredients and mix until smooth. Pour into the crust. Bake for 20 minutes. Cool. Re-set oven to 450 degrees F. Mix the sour cream with sugar and vanilla. Spread over the cheesecake. Bake for only 3 to 5 minutes. Refrigerate for at least 3 hours. Serves 12.

Nutritional Information: 90 Calories, 15 g Carbohydrate, 0 mg Cholesterol, 307 mg Sodium, 7 g Protein, 0 g Fiber.

ALMOND CLOUDS

2 egg whites, room temperature
1/3 C. sugar

1/3 C. almonds, toasted and finely
  chopped
1/2 t. almond extract

Preheat oven to 300 degrees F. Beat egg whites in a medium bowl until soft and peaks form. Gradually add the sugar, 1 tablespoon at a time, beating until soft peaks form. Fold in almonds and extract. Drop by heaping teaspoonfuls, 1 inch apart, onto waxed paper-lined cookie sheet. Bake for 35 minutes. Cool slightly on the cookie sheet. Remove gently from the waxed paper and cool completely on wire racks. Makes 42 cookies.

Nutritional Information Per Serving (1 Cookie): 14 Calories, 1 gm Fat, 2 g Carbohydrate, 0 mg Cholesterol, 3 mg Sodium, 0 gm Protein, 0 gm Dietary Fiber.

OATMEAL RASPBERRY BARS

1/3 C. margarine
2/3 C. brown sugar, firmly packed
1 t. vanilla
1 C. oatmeal, dry
1 C. flour
1/2 t. baking soda

1/4 t. salt
1-10 oz. pkg. frozen unsweetened
  raspberries
2 T. sugar
2 T. cornstarch
1/4 t. almond extract

Place margarine in a bowl and microwave until softened. Add the brown sugar and beat on high with an electric mixer for 5 minutes, or until creamy. Add the vanilla and mix well. Add the oatmeal, flour, baking soda and salt, stirring until mixture resembles coarse meal. Press 2 cups of the mixture in the bottom of an 8-inch glass square baking dish. Set aside the remaining flour mixture. Microwave at high for 3 minutes, or until the crust looks fluffed, rotating dish a half-turn after 1 1/2 minutes. Set aside. Microwave raspberries in their package on high for 2 minutes, or until thawed. Combine raspberries, sugar and cornstarch in a 2-cup glass measuring cup. Microwave at high for 2 1/2 minutes, or until thickened and bubbly, stirring after 1 1/2 minutes. Stir in the almond extract. Spread raspberry mixture over the crust. Top with remaining flour mixture. Microwave on high for 3 1/2 minutes to 3 minutes and 45 seconds, or until bubbly and top looks puffed, rotation dish a half-turn after 2 minutes. Let cool. Will make 16 servings.

Nutritional Information Per Serving (1 Bar): 134 Calories, 4 g Fat, 12 g Carbohydrate, 0 mg Cholesterol, 106 mg Sodium, 2 g Protein, 2 gm Dietary Fiber.

LEMONADE BARS

Crust:

1 1/2 C. flour

1/4 C. oatmeal

1 C. light margarine

1/2 C. powdered sugar

Topping:

1 C. egg substitute

2 C. sugar

1-6 oz. can undiluted lemonade

1/2 C. flour

1/2 t. baking powder

2 T. powdered sugar

Preheat oven to 325 degrees F. Spray a 9x13-inch pan with nonfat cooking spray. Blend the crust ingredients and pat into the pan. Bake for 20 minutes.

In a large bowl, combine the rest of the ingredients, except the powdered sugar. Use an electric mixer to mix well. Pour into the pan and bake for 25 to 30 minutes. Cool and cut into bars. Dust with the powdered sugar. Makes 24 bars.

Nutritional Information: 180 Calories, 5 g Fat, 0 g Saturated Fat, 33 g Carbohydrate, 0 mg Cholesterol, 25 mg Sodium, 3 g Protein, 1 g Fiber, 23 g Sugar.

OATMEAL MUFFINS

2 large egg whites
1/3 C. pure maple syrup
3 T. fresh orange juice
1 C. skim milk
1 T. vanilla extract
1 t. ground cinnamon
1/8 t. ground allspice
1/8 t. ground cloves

1/8 t. ground nutmeg
1 T. orange zest
1 1/2 C. rolled oats
1 C. whole wheat flour
1 t. baking powder
1/4 C. chopped pecans
1/4 C. dried cranberries

Preheat the oven to 350 degrees F. Spray a 12-hole muffin tin with vegetable oil. Put the egg whites in a large mixing bowl and whisk until frothy. Whisk in the next 9 ingredients. Stir in the flour and baking powder and mix. Fold in the pecans and cranberries. Fill the muffin tin 2/3-full. Bake for 20 minutes, or until the muffins are firm in the center. Makes 12 muffins.

Nutritional Information Per Serving (1 Muffin): 128 Calories, 2.5 g Fat.

Drink 'til he's cute.

BANANA BREAD

1 C. flour
1/2 C. whole wheat flour
1/2 C. sugar
2 t. baking powder
1 t. baking soda
1/4 t. salt
1 t. cinnamon

1 t. allspice
1/2 C. wheat germ
3 ripe bananas, mashed
1/2 C. low-fat buttermilk
3 T. vegetable oil
4 egg whites

Preheat oven to 350 degrees F. Spray a loaf pan with non-stick vegetable cooking spray. Stir together the first 9 ingredients. Add the remaining ingredients and stir until blended. Pour mixture into the loaf pan. Bake for 1 hour, or until done. Will make 16 slices.

Nutritional Information Per Serving (1 Slice): 125 Calories, 3 g Fat, 22 g Carbohydrate, 0 mg Cholesterol, 156 mg Sodium, 4 g Protein, 1 g Dietary Fiber.

WHITE CHOCOLATE MOUSSE

1-1 oz. pkg. white chocolate sugar-
    free, fat-free instant pudding mix
1 1/2 C. skim milk

1 1/2 C. frozen reduced-fat
    whipped topping, thawed
Fresh raspberries

Prepare pudding mix according to package directions using 1 1/2 cups skim milk. Fold the whipped topping into the pudding. Cover and chill at least 3 hours. Garnish with the raspberries. Serve 4.

Nutritional Information: 114 Calories, 3.1 g Fat, 3.1 g Saturated Fat, 15.7 g Carbohydrate, 2 mg Cholesterol, 232 mg Sodium, 3.7 g Protein, 0.6 g Dietary Fiber.

BREAD PUDDING

2 eggs
2 egg whites
1 1/2 C. skim milk

2 T. honey
1 t. vanilla
3 C. cubed raisin bread

Preheat the oven to 325 degrees F. Spray a 9-inch pie plate with a non-stick coating. Set aside. In a mixing bowl, add the eggs and egg whites and stir until combined. Beat in the milk, honey and vanilla. Stir in the bread cubes. Pour into the pie plate. Bake for 35 to 40 minutes. Let stand for 20 minutes. Serves 6.

Nutritional Information: 124 Calories, 3 g Total Fat, 1 g Saturated Fat, 18 g Carbohydrate, 72 mg Cholesterol, 139 mg Sodium, 7 g Protein, 0 g Fiber.

RASPBERRY SORBET

2 C. fresh or unsweetened frozen
  raspberries
2 T. fructose

1/2 C. unsweetened apple juice
2 t. orange liqueur

In a blender, combine the first 3 ingredients and process briefly. Strain through a fine sieve to remove the seeds. Stir in the liqueur. Pour in a small square pan and freeze. Serves 6.

Nutritional Information: 49 Calories, 0 g Fat, 11 g Carbohydrate, 0 mg Cholesterol, 1 mg Sodium, 0 g Protein, 1 g Fiber.

ORANGE SORBET

3 C. fresh squeezed orange juice   1/2 C. sugar

In a saucepan, combine 1/4 cup orange juice and the sugar. Boil over high heat, stirring, until sugar is dissolved, about 1 minute. Place in a shallow 2-quart dish and add remaining orange juice, stirring to mix. Freeze until solid, 2 to 3 hours. With a fork, break into small pieces and place in a food processor until smooth. Transfer to an airtight container and store in the freezer. Let soften in the refrigerator, 10 to 15 minutes, before serving. Serves 6.

Nutritional Information: 120 Calories, Trace Fat, Trace Saturated Fat, 1.8% Calories from Fat, 30 g Carbohydrate, 0 mg Cholesterol, 1 mg Sodium, 1 g Protein, Trace Dietary Fiber. Exchanges: 1 Fruit, 1 Other Carbohydrate.

BERRY TRIFLE

1/2-3 oz. pkg. ladyfingers, cubed
4 t. orange liqueur or orange juice
1 1/2 C. raspberries, blueberries
  and sliced strawberries
1 C. cubed red papaya

1-6 oz. carton vanilla fat-free
  yogurt with sweetener
1/4-8 oz. container frozen light
  whipped dessert topping,
  thawed

Divide the cubed ladyfingers among 4 dessert dishes. Drizzle with orange liqueur. Top with half of the berries and half of the papaya. In a small bowl, fold together yogurt and whipped topping. Spoon yogurt mixture on top of layers in the dishes. Top with the rest of the remaining berries and papaya. Serves 4.

Nutritional Information: 188 Calories, 3 g Total Fat, 2 g Saturated Fat, 22 g Carbohydrate, 39 mg Cholesterol, 38 mg Sodium, 4 g Protein, 4 g Fiber. Exchanges: 0.5 Fruit, 1 Carbohydrate, 0.5 Fat. Carb Choices: 1.5.

APPLE NACHOS

Gary Gardia, St. George, UT

2-6 inch whole wheat flour
  tortillas
1 t. sugar
1/2 t. apple pie spice
2 medium apples, sliced

1/2 C. water
1 T. packed brown sugar
1 T. raisins
1/2 t. finely-shredded orange peel

Preheat oven to 400 degrees F. Lightly coat both sides of the tortillas with the cooking spray. In a small bowl, combine the sugar and spice and sprinkle over the tortillas. Cut each tortilla into 6 wedges. Place in muffin cups. Bake wedges for 8 to 10 minutes, or until crisp. Cool on wire rack. In a large skillet, combine the rest of the ingredients. Bring to a boil and reduce heat. Cover and simmer about 5 minutes. Simmer, uncovered, another 5 minutes. Serve with the tortilla wedges. Makes 4 servings.

Nutritional Information: 133 Calories, 1 g Total Fat, 0 g Saturated Fat, 30 g Carbohydrate, 0 mg Cholesterol, 193 mg Sodium, 2 g Protein, 3 g Fiber. Exchanges: 1 Starch, 1 Fruit. Carb Choices: 2.

CARAMEL APPLE CRISP

1 lb. small cooking apples, cut into 1/2-inch slices, about 5 cups
1/4 C. low-calorie cranberry juice
1 t. finely-shredded lemon peel
1/4 t. ground allspice
1 C. low-fat granola

1/4 C. chopped pecans, toasted
1/4 C. fat-free caramel ice cream topping
Light or low-fat vanilla ice cream or frozen yogurt

In a 10-inch skillet, combine the apples, cranberry juice and lemon peel. Cook over medium-high for 6 to 8 minutes, stirring occasionally. Remove from the heat. Sprinkle apples with the allspice. Spoon apple mixture into 6 dessert dishes. Sprinkle with granola and nuts. Drizzle with caramel topping and spoon the ice cream on top. Serves 6.

Nutritional Information: 172 Calories, 4 g Total Fat, 1 g Saturated Fat, 34 g Carbohydrate, 0 mg Cholesterol, 76 mg Sodium, 2 g Protein, 3 g Fiber.

My greatest fear is that there is not PMS and this is my personality.

BAKED PUMPKIN CUSTARD

6 eggs
1/2 C. sugar
1-15 oz. can pumpkin
1/4 t. salt
1 t. ground cinnamon

1/2 t. ground ginger
1/4 t. ground cloves
3 C. skim milk, heated until very
  hot
Boiling water

Preheat oven to 350 degrees F. Adjust oven rack to center position. Spray 6-6 or 8 ounce custard cups with Pam. Set them into a large baking dish. In a large bowl, beat the egg slightly. Add the sugar, pumpkin, salt and the spices. Beat until combined. Mix in the hot milk until blended. Pour the egg mixture into the custard cups. Pour the hot water into the large baking pan to come halfway up the sides of the custard cups. Bake 25 to 30 minutes. When the center of the custard is just set, it will jiggle a little when shaken. Remove from oven and cool the custard cups on a wire rack. Cover with plastic wrap and refrigerate at least 2 hours. Serves 6.

Nutritional Information: 210 Calories, 6 g Fat.

FRUIT BAVARIAN

1-3 oz. pkg. strawberry gelatin
1 C. boiling water

2 C. fat-free frozen strawberry
  yogurt
1/4 C. brandy

Dissolve gelatin in the boiling water. Add the yogurt and stir until melted. Add the brandy. Pour into 4 serving dishes and chill until set. Serves 4.

Nutritional Information: 205 Calories, 38 g Carbohydrate, 0 mg Cholesterol, 104 mg Sodium, 5 g Protein, 0 g Dietary Fiber.

INDEX

NOTES

_____

_____

_____

_____

_____

_____

_____

_____

_____

_____

_____

_____

_____

_____

_____

_____

INDEX

BREAKFAST AND BREADS

APPETIZERS

SOUPS AND SALADS

MAIN MEALS

VEGETABLES

DESSERTS

NOTES & RECIPES

_____

_____

_____

_____

_____

_____

_____

_____

_____

_____

_____

_____

_____

_____

_____

_____

_____

THE COOKBOOK CO.

ANY BITCH CAN COOK

ANY BITCH CAN PARTY

ANY BITCH CAN DRINK

SUGAR BITCHES

ANY BITCH CAN FAKE IT

ANY BITCH CAN SALSA

MERRY BITCHIN HOLIDAYS

EAT BITCH & WINE

ANY QUEEN CAN DECORATE

ANY BITCH CAN HEAT IT UP

BITCHIN & GRILLIN

ANY BITCH CAN TOSS IT

ANY BITCH CAN LOSE IT

www.anybitchcookbooks.com